They called it

THE BILLION DOLLAR COPPER CAMP...

During a period of seventy years, the men that ruled Jerome mined and smelted more than a billion dollars worth of metals. At the peak of its prosperity, Jerome's proud citizens called this sprawling mining camp "The Billion Dollar Copper Camp" and "The Most Unique City in America."

Then, when the last of its known commercial ore deposits were exhausted, Jerome suddenly ceased its existence as a mining center, and as described by its remaining handful of residents, became "The Largest Ghost City in America."

In *Ghosts of Cleopatra Hill*, Herbert V. Young has told a fascinating story of life in the early days of this historic mining community, of the men that discovered its immense mineral deposits and sold them for a song, of the more fortunate men that developed them, and of those with ready guns that tried to uphold the law.

The Jerome Historical Society originally published this book in 1964 when Jerome was a virtual ghost town. Most buildings mentioned as vacant have since been restored. Many of the people that Young indicated as living have since passed away.

GHOSTS
of Cleopatra Hill

Men and Legends of Old Jerome

ABOUT THE AUTHOR

Herbert V. Young was born in 1887 at Brushwood Manor, his parents' Arizona homestead. It was located 15 miles north of the village of Phoenix, in what is now Scottsdale.

After finishing a business college course, Young engaged in secretarial work. From 1912–1955, Young was secretary to the general manager of Jerome's United Verde Copper Company (purchased by Phelps Dodge Corporation in 1931).

He started writing in his seventies, drawing upon 43 years of experience in the development and decline of Jerome's mining operations. His two books about Jerome's mining history were published by the Jerome Historical Society: *Ghosts of Cleopatra Hill* (1964) and *They Came to Jerome* (1972).

In 1983, Northland Press of Flagstaff, Arizona published *Water by the Inch,* Young's reminiscences about his pioneer family and boyhood adventures on their desert homestead.

Young was a founding member of the Jerome Historical Society and served as its historian from 1953 until his death in 1988. He donated his papers and photographs to the Jerome Historical Society, which has archived them as The Herbert V. Young collection.

GHOSTS
of Cleopatra Hill

Men and Legends of Old Jerome

BY HERBERT V. YOUNG

Jerome Historical Society
Jerome, Arizona

BOOKS BY HERBERT V. YOUNG

Ghosts of Cleopatra Hill
They Came to Jerome
Water by the Inch

Sixth printing, 2001 with new chapter 24 and index

Published and distributed by:
The Jerome Historical Society
P.O. Box 156
Jerome, AZ 86331

Cover design by Sullivan Santamaria Design, Inc.

Index by James Steinberg

Library of Congress Catalog Card No. 64-8658

ISBN 0-9621000-5-6

Printed in the United States of America

TO MY WIFE "ZIP"
ZELIA SEAMAN YOUNG

*A faithful partner for more than
half a century*

CONTENTS

INTRODUCTION

Ten years ago I had the pleasure of writing the introduction which appeared in the six editions already published of Herbert V. Young's historical book on Jerome, GHOSTS OF CLEOPATRA HILL. Now the book is being re-published with the addition of new material, and I am doubly pleased to have been invited to write an introduction to the new edition.

This book has certainly lived up to everything we had hoped for it. It has enjoyed wide distribution, with copies in libraries as far away as New York, London and Australia.

GHOSTS OF CLEOPATRA HILL deals mainly with the rich mines which were responsible for the fame of Jerome and the men who found and developed the mines. Only Herb could have written it, as not only did he know most of the people he described so well, he worked closely with many of them. He has captured the true feeling of the early days and the people who played such an important part in building the area we old-timers loved so much. There is no question that this book has brought a closer tie among us who are left from this unique mining community. Perhaps it will help to explain the bond that exists between the people who have lived in Jerome throughout the years.

The success of GHOSTS OF CLEOPATRA HILL led to the publication of another book, THEY CAME TO JEROME, which tells of the unique town of Jerome itself and the people who built it, then rebuilt it again and again. These people saw it develop, expand, and finally die as a mining community, only to return in a new identity, that of a famous tourist attraction. Jerome now enjoys fame as the best known occupied ghost town in the world.

The Jerome Historical Society and the author are to be thanked and congratulated for having contributed such a valuable addition to the history of Arizona as GHOSTS OF CLEOPATRA HILL.

LEWIS J. McDONALD
Executive Director of University Relations
Northern Arizona University
Flagstaff, Arizona

AUTHOR'S FOREWORD
to the 1974 enlarged editions

As this is written, nearly a decade has passed since the first of the six previous editions of GHOSTS OF CLEOPATRA HILL was published. Now a generous public has called for still another printing.

During the past ten years research into Jerome's history has been continued. Through the resurgence of interest in this unique mining community which this book helped to create, contact has been made with men and women who were able to furnish biographical material concerning a number of the earlier mining men of the Verde district which I had not previously discovered. Old newspapers, magazine and historical writings have been valuable sources.

Largely because of the great publicity it has received there have been many changes in Jerome during the past decade. The population has increased. Most of the old and vacant residence buildings which were not dismantled, moved to other areas, or demolished by ground movement, are now occupied, and restoration is being conducted on others. This is obvious to the tourist approaching Jerome from either direction—but this should be borne in mind: The structures in the business section of the old city, that section which confronts the visitor on making pause, are being maintained as nearly as possible as they were when there was no question about Jerome being "THE largest ghost city in America." The city government, the Jerome Historical Society, and the several other organizations dedicated to preserving Jerome's heritage are determined to keep it that way.

In 1967 the Department of the Interior of the United States designated Jerome as a National Historic Landmark. The Douglas mansion at the United Verde Extension mine site was presented to the State of Arizona by the Douglas family, and under the jurisdiction of the State Parks Board a fine museum was established there. This, with the museum of the Jerome Historical Society and the many other attractions helps to bring visitors to Jerome from all over the world. They find much to entertain and instruct. But not the least of the things which the visitor will long remember is outside the confines of the city itself: It is when, standing on Jerome's mountainside and fronting eastward, they see that grand and glorious panorama of Nature's handiwork which is the Verde Valley, with its ever changing moods and colors, stretching away for innumerable miles while ever rising to the rim of the far plateau.

—HERBERT V. YOUNG

AUTHOR'S FOREWORD
to 1964, 1966 and 1968 editions

Like any community which has had its birth in rugged isolation, Jerome in its early days was peopled by a hardy breed of men. Its development was financially primed by adventurers of another class, who, inspired by the romance of mining or by greed, were ready and willing to make wager at Fortune's wheel.

In the writing of this book it has been my intent to picture as accurately as possible those who played the principal parts in locating, promoting and developing the ore deposits and the town they sustained; of two whose connection with the camp speeded their way toward national and international prominence in the political field, and of three men of the law whose work in keeping the peace led to deeds the echoes of which still lurk in legend, and which gave them more than local fame.

The materials for this work have been drawn from many sources. First comes my own experiences during residence in the Verde Valley for more than half a century, and my close contact with most of the characters pictured. The minds of scores of old timers have been explored for facts and fables. The writings of many reporters and historians have been studied. From these founts have been drawn the amalgam of fact, legend and fiction which makes up the book.

I regret that my memory is not long enough, nor my records complete enough, to enable me to give individual credits for all sources I have drawn upon over the years spent in collecting material, but I do extend sincerest thanks to the many pioneers and writers who have been of help to me.

— HERBERT V. YOUNG

Overlooking the United Verde's Open Pit in the early 1920's.
Photo by Frank Staley, Collection Jerome Historical Society.

Beautiful and Ugly

PORTRAIT OF JEROME

First a tent town, quickly a roaring mining camp, and finally a ghost city, Jerome sprawls dilapidated and tired on the eastern slope of Cleopatra Hill. What impressions it has made or what memories it evokes depends upon the time a visitor was there, what he did and whom he met, and the depth of his perceptions and sensibilities.

An opinion of Jerome might have been developed by the accident of living there, by impressions received while passing through, or by one's feeling for beauty, ugliness, enterprise, sin or romance. Some reacted to its virtues, some to its faults, others to the grandeur of its setting.

This cliff-hanging, mile-high community in the Black Mountains of central Arizona has been a place of many faces, and these have been viewed from many angles. It was the jewel of the Verde Valley, or the canker of Cleopatra Hill; a model mining city, or a rough and savage frontier camp infested by drifters, killers, gamblers and tarts; a community of churches, schools, charitable societies and happy homes, or a decadent rookery of saloons, dens and cribs; a region of magnificent scenery and invigorating air, or a place of desolate surroundings and stinking, corroding fumes which debased it to the status of a suburb of hell.

In early days the many faces created many problems. The wealth of Jerome's fabulously rich mineral deposits attracted men from east, west, north and south, below and above the borders and beyond the several seas — from wherever men had attained the skills, the ambitions or the hungers which they hoped to make use of in garnering a share of the community's free-flowing cash. People of opposing nationalities, traits, creeds and customs were of necessity intermingled, willingly or not. They hated, fought, and often killed.

Other problems were characteristic of all bonanza mining camps. The hangers-on were in abundance; gamblers and bandits, cheats and gay women, and the inevitable complement, the tough and straight-shooting lawmen.

This mining camp of international fame was built precariously on the eastern slope of the Verde Valley's high western wall, of which lofty Mingus Mountain is the grim and rugged sentinel. At the valley's lowest elevation the Verde River twists its green path southward. Above Jerome's decadent buildings towers the tall black cone known as Cleopatra Hill. Once the hill was covered with oak and pine, but for more than sixty years its steep and rugged slopes have been bare, denuded of vegetation by the acid fumes of the copper smelter which for two decades growled at Cleopatra's northern foot.

Now where the smelter once sprawled are the scarred walls of a gaping pit six hundred feet deep, from which huge power shovels gouged millions of tons of overburden and rich ores. Downward for five thousand feet beneath the pit and the surrounding slopes is a honey-comb of shafts, drifts, winzes and stopes — a hundred miles of them, now waterfilled and caving. During the town's boom days Jerome became the third largest city in Arizona; within it and over the ridges and up and down adjoining canyons and gulches, fifteen thousand inhabitants lived. The core of these activities lay in the morning glare and evening shadows of Cleopatra Hill.

In this day, when most of Jerome's streets are quiet and buildings are crumbling, only memories and scanty records can be drawn upon to sketch a picture of the raucous mining camp which its early residents knew. Much of Jerome's fascinating history can not be found in available records or material. The old town had several newspapers at various periods; The Jerome Chronicle, The Jerome Mining News, the Jerome Reporter, the Jerome Hustler, the Jerome Copper Belt, the Jerome Sun and the Verde Copper News—the latter a daily during the town's most active years. Only incomplete files of these publications exist.

In the days when Jerome was a group of wooden shacks and tents, Tombstone had already been branded throughout the country as an infamously sinful town to be avoided by the timid and the good. The glamour it has gained through the years did not surround it then. In

2

counteraction, Jerome endeavored to establish for itself an image of a sinless, model community, inhabited and guided by honest men and pure women. It played down its killings and other crimes inevitable in a wealthy mining camp where an abundance of money had attracted to it a high percentage of gamblers, drifters, tough workmen and harlots from all the rough camps of the West. An editorial in an early-day issue of the Jerome Reporter included this comment:

> . . . . There is practically no crime in Jerome. Deeds of violence are almost unknown.

If the editor had a conscience it must have hurt him. In a later year a former resident of Jerome who had lived in the camp during its most active days reported that he had seen eight shootings in one year's time — and he hadn't seen them all — to say nothing of the quieter knifings and acts of mayhem which spilled blood in many sections of Jerome. "Deeds of violence" were unknown only to the extent that they were not heralded to the outside world. The watchfulness of Jim Roberts, Fred Hawkins, John Hudgens, and other marshals and deputies with keen eyes and ready guns retarded violence but by no means subdued it.

For half a century the people of Jerome lived in the belief that the town and its mines could never die, reflecting the optimism of Senator William A. Clark of Montana, principal owner of the great United Verde mine during the larger share of its life. "The mine's ore bodies are claimed to be practically inexhaustible," said the Jerome Reporter. "Generations of Clarks two centuries hence may be reaping dividends from the United Verde."

Senator Clark had been free in expressing that hope. He still held it at his death in 1925. He commanded his sons and daughters never to part with this favorite of his many enterprises.

Ten years later the Clark heirs had fought themselves out of ownership. In another fifteen years the great mine was dead.

Jerome's Main Street in Boom Days.

Jerome's Main Street circa 1965, its buildings empty, wrecked or gone.

Before and After

HISTORICAL BRIEF

Though early historians of the American West only presumed that the mineral deposits on the eastern slope of the Black Mountains of Arizona's central section may have been visited by Spanish explorers in the sixteenth century, Katherine Bartlett, Curator of History of the Museum of Northern Arizona, has ably demonstrated that they did. ("Notes upon the Routes of Espejo and Farfan to the Mines in the Sixteenth Century," New Mexico Historical Review, January, 1942.) Antonio de Espejo in 1583 and Marcos Farfan in 1598 each claimed them in the name of the Spanish crown.

Following these visits no white man is known to have set foot on the copper outcroppings until after the arrival in the Verde Valley in 1865 of American settlers from Prescott. A cavalry post was established at Fort Verde to protect the settlers, under the command successively of Generals Crook and Miles. Attached to the cavalry troop was Al Sieber, noted scout and guide; learning of the copper deposits from his Indian guides, legend has it, he staked a claim there, but was too busy to record it.

In 1876 a group of prospectors located ten claims and a millsite. They drove some short tunnels and shallow shafts. Fearful that the rich ore they had exposed was only surface showing, they were ready to sell when potential purchasers arrived. Frederick A. Tritle, soon to become territorial governor, acquired an interest in some of the claims and in 1882 assisted in the organization of the United Verde Copper Company — a name which in the following half century was to become one of the most famous in the mining world. For less than one hundred thousand dollars the promoters bought the interests of the locators. The camp was named Jerome in honor of Eugene Jerome of New York, secretary and manager of the enterprise.

The Atlantic and Pacific Railroad was then moving westward across Arizona. A wagon road was built to rail at Ash Fork, and a small smelter was freighted in by mule team. Rich matte was produced in 1883 and 1884; then, due to a decline in the price of copper and a decrease in the metal content of the ores, financial difficulties developed and the smelter was closed. In 1887 Frederick Tritle leased the properties and smelted some copper, but suffered heavy loss.

Dr. James Douglas of Phelps, Dodge and Company's Copper Queen interests then began negotiations for a lease and option on the property, but no agreement was reached. William A. Clark of Montana stepped in early in 1888 and optioned a large majority of the stock. He developed bonanza ore bodies, reopened the little smelter, and shipped his product out and supplies in by wagon road across the Black Mountains connecting with a railroad which had been built under territorial subsidy from Seligman to Prescott. In the early nineties Clark built his own narrow gauge road into Jerome and constructed a smelter with a capacity of five millions pounds of copper monthly.

Due to the discovery of extensive new ore bodies and the settling of the ground on which the smelter was located, this plant was abandoned in 1915 and smelting begun at the huge new ore reduction works at Clarkdale on the Verde River, four miles from Jerome and 2,000 feet lower.

Clark, a United States senator from Montana during the first six years of the century, was sole operator of the United Verde until his death in 1925. Because of dissatisfactions due to the closing of the mine and smelter in the depression years of the early thirties, quarreling among the heirs, and a belief that the world would be over-supplied with copper for a century to come, members of the family holding a majority of the shares decided to sell. Phelps Dodge Corporation acquired control in 1935.

When Clark took over in 1888 Jerome's first boom began. Shacks and tents were replaced by more substantial structures. Three devastating fires were followed by the building of larger and more substantial structures. The town continued to grow slowly until the explosion set off by the discovery of the United Verde Extension bonanza in 1914. This property, known as the UVX or Little Daisy, was headed by James S. Douglas, son of the man who was outbid by Clark for the United Verde. The UVX was mined out in 1938, after producing more than one hundred million dollars in copper, gold and silver.

At its best, Jerome was a small city of substantial buildings, many of them made of stone, brick and concrete. There were many good homes, some fine ones. Prior to the decline of the mines, the business section of

BEFORE AND AFTER

Jerome was harassed by slippage of surface ground on the steep slopes and by mining underneath. This condition caused the disintegration of many of these buildings. Rising tier on tier up the steep slopes of Cleopatra Hill and dropping down to the gulches, most of the structures which were left became empty shells. The town's center suffered the most; many of the larger buildings are gone, victims of the ground movement and the wreckers.

One of the more solid of the remaining structures is the one which houses the exhibits of the mine museum of the Jerome Historical Society, once the more than locally famous Fashion Saloon. Here one may find the story of the vanished mines which for seventy years gave prosperity to Jerome and other communities of the Verde Valley. Exhibits fill the space where once dancing girls gave entertainment to the hard rock miners and furnacemen. Only a block away, around a corner and down a slope, is the long line of vacant rooms of the quarter known as "the cribs".

On a lower street rises the empty concrete shell of a six-story hotel. One level above Main Street a once handsome building containing commodious apartments stands in gloomy emptiness, and high to the south looms the large hospital which for many years served all of Northern Arizona, but now long closed.

From Jerome one has a breath-taking view of the Verde Valley and the carved and terraced red rocks thirty miles to the east — a view which rivals the Grand Canyon in magnificence. Nestled among the sculptures at the lower end of gorgeous Oak Creek Canyon is the beautiful community of Sedona, with its unmatched setting and many fine homes. Dozens of motion pictures have been filmed in this famous red rock area. A few miles below Sedona is Cornville, a picturesque settlement with a picturesque name, where lived Frank Gyberg, sage of the cattle camps and well known stockman, writer and humorist.

Much closer, on a hill by the Verde River, are the excavated ruins of the multi-roomed pueblo of Tuzigoot, a center of aboriginal life seven hundred to a thousand years ago and now a national monument.

Down the mountain on a lower level and east of the town is the United Verde Extension mine area, where a headframe marks the location of the shaft through which a hundred million dollars worth of copper ores were hoisted. Nearby is the mansion, built by James S. Douglas, whose heirs have given this handsome structure to the State of Arizona. It is now a public museum administered by the State Parks Board.

GHOSTS OF CLEOPATRA HILL

At Clarkdale are the scabby remains of the smelter which for thirty-six years steamed and smoked in the process of extracting two thousand million pounds of copper to feed the metal markets of the world. Here gold and silver and zinc were also produced in quantity. Next to the smelter, thrusting into the river channel and altering the stream's course, is the huge slag dump which received thirty million tons of molten waste, rich in iron yet to be recovered.

South of Clarkdale the buildings of the spreading pioneer town of Cottonwood are seen nestling among the green trees which mark the twisting course of the Verde River.

Though badly hurt, Clarkdale did not die with the closing of the smelter. It has maintained existence as an attractive community of homes. Nearby is the modern plant of the Phoenix Cement Company, which furnished the cement for the Glen Canyon dam.

When the big mine and smelter closed, Phelps Dodge found places for many of the employees in its other Arizona operations. As the town emptied, the few citizens who had no other place to go watched the exodus with the feeling that the world as they had known it was coming to an end. The late James Brewer, then superintendent of Tuzigoot National Monument, saw the possibility of making a tourist attraction of the dying town which had once proudly called itself the "Billion Dollar Copper Camp" and the "Most Unique City in America". Spurred on by Brewer, the citizens organized the Jerome Historical Society, established a museum, and advertised itself as "The Largest Ghost City in America."

Another attraction of which the Society became a sponsor was the art gallery opened by the Verde Valley Artists, which soon became well known throughout the Southwest and beyond.

The 1970 census takers counted 293 people in Jerome. Even so, a few of Jerome's residents claim that "Ghost City" is a misnomer. More than half a million tourists visited Jerome in the first ten years of the Society's existence, but after viewing the wreckage of a once great mine, the many empty buildings, and the rubble-strewn lots where substantial structures once stood, only a few have seemed ready to doubt that there are more ghosts than living people in this shattered mining camp, this "city of Romantic Ruins."

*Jerome and United Verde Smelter about 1900. Big Montana Hotel looms
in upper center.*

*When the mines closed, Jerome became a celebrated ghost town.
Restoration began in the early 1970's.*

JEROME
POPULATION
~~15,000~~
~~10,000~~
~~5,000~~
~~1,000~~
GHOST CITY

*Excavated ruins of Tuzigoot Pueblo. Earliest known inhabitants of
Verde Valley lived here about seven hundred years ago.*

Men of Spain

THE FIRST EXPLORERS

As the rough ascending trail leveled out on a long ridge two thousand feet above the river flats, Captain Antonio de Espejo turned in his saddle. He took a moment to inspect the tumbled land which lay beneath him and beyond the river.

"Magnifico!" the captain breathed. The word was subdued; he must display no sentimental front to his hard companions.

They had climbed two thousand feet up from the river, and beneath them lay the wide valley's variegated pattern of grays, browns and greens. Thirty miles beyond the river and forming the eastern wall of the valley arose weird structures of red sandstone, carved by the elements into fantastic designs.

Reluctantly the captain urged his horse onward.

It was a motley procession which occupied the trail, a footpath really, which had taken them three miles from the river. In the lead strutted a breach-clouted young Indian, proud that he had been chosen to guide these white gods from another world. Next with a pack mule came the five horsemen, dressed in the worn garb of Spanish soldiers. In single file to the rear trailed a ragged line of native mountain people, whose curiosity to learn why the visitors were interested in their mine was stronger than their fear.

From the ridge the trail snaked upward along the slopes of a small, rocky canyon. It was cool up there, where tall and fragrant pines replaced the juniper, mesquite and cactus of the lower elevations.

The guide paused and pointed to a pile of loose rock which spilled downward over the slope.

"It is the mine," announced the leader of the cavalcade.

They tethered their horses and mules in a growth of jack pine, and took a narrow path which wound up and around the rock pile. At the

11

end of the path was a leveled spot, from which a tunnel, partially blocked by fallen boulders, led into the hill.

"But small sign of riches here," declared the older of the Spaniards.

"Make not judgment in haste, Luxan. First let us see what is beyond the tunnel mouth."

He beckoned to the natives; several men came forward and with eager hands cleared the debris away.

"Hernandez, a taper from your pack."

When the taper was lit the captain ordered his aide into the tunnel, and when it was reported safe Espejo followed. Some distance from the portal they found a low roofed stope where brightly colored rock gleamed in the taper's light. Stone hammers and picks were scattered on the floor.

At the captain's order Hernandez broke from the wall several pieces of the glistening rock, and they returned to daylight. Espejo displayed the ore to his men. In the sun it glowed with colors of peacock brilliance.

"A large vein of this ore has been opened. It is heavy with metal."

"But with copper only — would you not say in truth?" Luxan retorted. "Where are the colors of silver, or of gold?"

"It is a mine of great richness," Espejo insisted. "We will take possession."

At his order two small crosses were constructed of poles and thong. One was set up in the stope, the other near the tunnel.

"Hernandez, Barreto, de Luna — your arms!"

The three men made ready their harquebuses.

"In the name of God and the King," the captain proclaimed. Briefly he prayed.

"Make ready. Fire!"

Flame and smoke belched thunderously from the muzzles of the guns. The guide squalled with fright and bounded away; the Indians who had followed the cavalcade scattered like quail, yelling and moaning in terror.

Thus, in late afternoon on the eighth day of May, in the year of our Lord fifteen hundred and eighty three, Antonio de Espejo, captain by commission from the viceroy of New Spain, claimed possession of the ground which three centuries later was to become one of the world's bonanza mines.

What caused these men to come dangerously many hundreds of miles to the little Indian mine in the unknown wilderness?

They were inspired by a curious mixture of urges, pride, ambition, patriotism, religious fervor, and in the case of Espejo himself by the hope that a great accomplishment could earn him pardon from the penalty of murder.

Coming from Spain, Antonio de Espejo and a brother became cattlemen and merchants in the Queretaro country of Mexico. In a fight between them and some of their hands a herdsman was killed, and the brothers were brought to trial and convicted of murder. The brother was jailed and Antonio was levied a heavy fine; rather than pay it he sought refuge in Chihuahua.

At the time two missionary priests who had traveled to the northern Rio Grande valley were reported to be in danger. Antonio felt that if he could rescue them he might win forgiveness for his crime. With fourteen armed men, a priest and Indian guides he set out in November, 1582. When the expedition reached its destination it was learned that the priests had been murdered.

Espejo felt they could not go home without evidence of some accomplishment, so he ordered the expedition westward in search of silver. When they reached the Hopi pueblos they learned of the mines to the south, and taking four men Espejo set out in search of them.

To justify his trip Espejo wrote enthusiastically about the mines and the richness of the ores. Diego Perez de Luxan, chronicler of the expedition, wrote in his journal that the ores were of copper and poor.

In 1598 Marcos de los Godos Farfan led another expedition to the mines, located many claims, and wrote glowingly of the fine mineral ledges and the great pastures and plains below, the fine lands for cultivation, and the abundance of water. When the American prospectors came in 1876 traces of the old workings on the outcroppings were still visible, and in one of the ancient stopes stone implements were found and, to the surprise of the prospectors who knew nothing of the Spanish visitations, a crumbling wooden cross.

One wonders at the seeming indifference of the early Spanish writers to the magnificent scenery encountered along their routes. If anything could have stirred the fancy and thrilled the hearts of these hard men it might have been the view to the east as they stood on the high slopes of the Black Mountains. When the little party left the mines the afternoon sun was slanting its rays toward the gorgeous red rocks carved by the elements through the ages to a thousand fanciful shapes, which formed the eastern wall of the multi-hued bowl which is now known as the upper Verde Valley. There appeared to be battlemented castles there, and cathedrals domed and spired, all limned in purple shade, the patterns ever changing as the clouds sailed beneath the sun and carried with them their moving shadows. It seems quite evident that these hardened explorers considered the recording of any emotional experiences beneath their dignity.

Yet that the men of the party must have been impressed Luxan gives an indication. Though the stream which twisted its way along the bottom of the wide valley was small as rivers go, and though Espejo and his companions had followed much larger ones they gave it the noble name of "El Rio de los Reyes"— the River of the Kings.

Jerome in the 1920s from Sunshine Hill. (Jerome Historical Society, Payne Col.)

Montezuma Castle, ancient Indian cliff dwelling near Camp Verde.

The American Pioneers

THE FIRST SETTLERS

Prescott, forty miles west of the Verde Valley and first settled by a hardy group of gold seekers, became the jumping off place for explorations in all directions after the first territorial government was established there in 1864. The town and the nearby military establishment of Fort Whipple became a good market for agricultural products, and those more interested in farming than in mining set their eyes to the green valley to the east, where rich lands and an abundance of water lay waiting.

Settlement of the valley had been discouraged by the military commanders at Fort Whipple, as they had their hands full guarding the new capital and the increasing influx of settlers and wanted no distant responsibilities. The aggressiveness of the Apaches increased with distance.

Despite the warnings, early in 1865 white settlers moved into the Verde Valley and prepared to farm acreages in the neighborhood of the present town of Camp Verde. The Indian menace was found to be present and very real, and in response to pleas for protection a garrison was ordered to the harassed settlement. Early in 1866 they established Camp Lincoln on the Verde. Later barracks were built on a more permanent basis at Fort Verde. These buildings still stand, and an interesting museum containing exhibits reminiscent of the post's military period has been established within them.

The garrison was active during the greater part of the succeeding decade before the valley finally became safe from Indian attack. Then more settlers flowed in, inspired by rosy tales of the good free land, fine water and lush ranges. Rich bottom lands were found to the north of the fort for twenty-five miles, and to the south and eastward along the Verde's permanently flowing tributaries — Oak Creek, Beaver Creek and Clear Creek.

The valley in those days could not have been much different in appearance than when Espejo and Farfan viewed it in 1583 and 1598, but it was far different than now. How different was told to me by

Across the Wide Valley. Red Rocks of Oak Creek Canyon east of Jerome.

Charles Douglas Willard, who as an adult resided continuously longer in the Verde Valley than has any other man.

Pioneer Willard was born in California and died in Cottonwood in 1957 at the age of 99. Arriving in the valley in 1879, he saw the first few shafts and drifts being driven on the outcrops in the Black Mountains where the Indians had mined centuries before; he saw and knew the first locators who had the courage to explore even though there could be little hope of financial profit for years to come. He saw the first smelting of United Verde ores in 1883, and the big mine abandoned in 1953. And after that he saw, with far less despair than most, the gloom of a group of communities whose inhabitants feared that, as copper had been their life, financial oblivion was near.

This is the way Charlie Willard told of his arrival and life in the Verde Valley:

My father and his five sons, of which I was the youngest, started horseback the long trip from Pine Valley, Nevada, in September of 1879, driving a herd of cattle and horses. The trip was a tough one, and we lost many cattle along the way. The greatest tragedy of the trip was our father's death of pneumonia in December.

Upper Verde River. Lush vegetation was typical of early days.

Late in January my brothers and I drove down from the northwest into the Verde Valley. The mountains around us had snow on them, but there was none in the valley. Down the center of the valley a wide band of trees up to a quarter of a mile wide marked the course of the river as far as the eye could see. Grass belly-high to a horse covered the hills and mesas, some of it still green despite the winter weather. Game, from quail to deer, was abundant. We had found a rancher's and hunter's paradise and knew the valley would be our home.

We located some good acreage and helped to start a little settlement we named Cottonwood. Many settlers followed us. Almost all of them brought horses and cattle, and within twenty years of the time the first white settlers came over from Prescott the ranges began to be over-grazed. The grass was eaten down, the ground packed, and no longer was there heavy vegetation to hold the water back until the ground could absorb it. Flood waters began cutting at the river's banks; the beaver dams which had been plentiful were washed out and the river bottom was scoured.

The Indians were gone when we arrived — the Apaches had been moved to the San Carlos reservation a year or two before. But we saw plenty of signs of the early inhabitants of the valley. There were ruins

19

of cliff dwellings and pueblos all up and down the river, and farther away there had been springs. In the red rocks where I homesteaded in later years there is an overhanging bluff beneath which there are two large ruins. In one of these ruins, scattered among rubble two or three feet deep, I found many human bones and wisps of hair, showing that a number of people had died in that one room — perhaps killed by Apache invaders. Every room had been set on fire.

These early inhabitants, as demonstrated by the excavations at Tuzigoot, lived in the valley for generations, leading a peaceful agricultural life. It is supposed that when the Apaches came the original inhabitants were either killed or driven away. Those who lived are believed to have gone to the pueblos in northern Arizona.

After we came to the valley some of the Apaches who had been moved to reservations escaped and came back, probably because they were homesick, and caused a few scares. But their marauding days were over, and they knew it. They were allowed to stay, and a reservation was set up for them north of Camp Verde. They settled down, some got jobs, and many of their children and grandchildren became useful citizens.

When I arrived in the valley in 1879 many mining claims had been located in the Black Mountains and a small camp had been established. As the camp grew I found a market for ranch and dairy products there. I knew all the early mining men and merchants. All of them are gone now.

Cottonwood (c. 1915)   FROM THE COLLECTION OF FRED

Bridegroom Charley Willard — 1890

Dr. James Douglas

Big Deal

THE FIRST SALE OF CLAIMS

It was cold at the little mile-high mining camp that Tuesday morning in December. A light snow covered the slopes, but not deeply enough to stay the rider from Fort Verde who each week came up the trail with the mail.

Down at the eastern foot of Cleopatra Hill a half mile below the mine workings, where the ground leveled off a bit, a few tents had been set up. In the larger of these one could purchase the more necessary items of food, and also some of the stuff that warmed and cheered. A small group of men had gathered here, among them Arthur Whitaker, who had come up from his camp in Mescal Gulch to pick up his mail. Angus McKinnon, too, had dropped down from his camp on the Wade Hampton claim.

At ten o'clock the rider from the Fort arrived with a light pouch of mail and one telegram, which bore lettering showing it had come to Fort Verde over the army's telegraph line.

"For Whitaker," the rider announced.

Whitaker received the envelope with a sense of foreboding. Telegrams usually meant bad news. The assembled miners waited silently, mentally assembling words of sympathy. They showed relief as they saw Whitaker's face light up.

"Good news, Art?" McKinnon asked.

"Maybe. Listen: This was sent from Maricopa down on the Southern Pacific railroad yesterday. 'Leaving on Prescott stage today to inspect mines   George Treadwell with me   Ask McKinnon and Ruffner to meet me at camp Wednesday'.   It's signed James Douglas."

"Who's Douglas?" McKinnon asked.

"I've heard George Treadwell, who's a friend of mine, speak of him," Whitaker answered. "He's been running a copper refinery in Pennsylvania, using a new method he invented. Professor, they call him — sometimes it's Doctor — he has a college degree of some kind."

"Has he got money?"

"I've heard he has rich associates, anyhow."

McKinnon arranged with the rider to deliver a note to Ruffner at his camp on the Verde, where he and his wife Sarah lived and where he spent most of his time during the cold season.

Ruffner and McKinnon were partners in the Wade Hampton claim, while Ruffner and his wife had located the Eureka. These claims, together with the Chrome South and Chrome North, directly to the east of the Eureka and Hampton, were the claims on which the most extensive outcroppings had been found.

Ruffner arrived at the camp early the next morning, and with McKinnon anxiously awaited the man who, with good luck, might relieve them of the strain of hanging on. For the past four years the claims had caused them many worries and had run them into debt.

"Andy, if Douglas offers to buy, will you sell?" McKinnon asked.

"Yes, if I get enough to pay off Richards and Head and the rest of them and have a decent stake left. My wife wants us to get out — I have to leave her alone too much."

"Rod and I feel about the same." Rod was Angus McKinnon's brother, who for his aid and financial support had been given an interest in the Wade Hampton. "I've been afraid for some time that the ore in the shaft and tunnel might run out."

"I've been worryin' a bit myself."

"What price will we ask?"

"How about fifteen thousand? It'll take about forty-five hundred to pay off the bills, and that would leave about thirty-five hundred for each of the three of us."

"Okay. But with the name of Douglas this fellow's probably Scotch — we'd better start our dickering with a higher offer. If we sell, will you go back South?"

"And be ruled by the damyankees? Not on your life. And I'll bet you won't go back to Nova Scotia, either."

"Rod and I are thinkin' of Mexico."

It had been a tough five years' grind since the claims on the side of the Black Mountains had been located in 1876, but it was a hard working bunch who had made the eight locations which lay in the heart of the mineral showings. Ruffner, christened Morris Andrew, was a Confederate veteran of the Civil War, and in the bitterness of defeat had

24

come west to get away from the devastation and heartaches which had been the inevitable aftermath of the great conflict. So too had come John Boyd, who had been a captain in the Confederate army and had located the Azure South claim below the Ruffner and McKinnon claims.

Then there were the Irishmen — the three O'Dougherty brothers, Ed, John, and A. B. John Kelley, Josiah Riley, and George Kell were the locators, singly or in groups, of the Chrome North and Chrome South, and the Azure North. Among these were men of skill; John O'Dougherty, called Doctor, had medical training; his brother Ed was an assayer, and others of the group knew well how to sharpen a drill or timber a shaft.

Adding to the hardships of the miners had been the difficulty of getting supplies. These had to be freighted to Fort Verde from Prescott, then transported to the claims by pack train. Thus the men got their tents, powder and tools, and such food as they could not kill on the forested mountain side or grassy flats or buy from the ranchers along the river.

The labor of the miners had not been confined to the assessment work; tunnels and shafts had been driven on the outcroppings, the continuing richness of the ore being the bait which kept the men at work. Yet there was always the fear that the ore in the tunnels would "peter out," or that sinking too energetically might "knock the bottom out" of the shafts.

There had been little hard cash in the group; it had been necessary to go into debt for supplies, and the Prescott men Ruffner had named, banker Hugo Richards and merchant Charles P. Head, after examining the claims had advanced money and supplies to keep the men at work, thus receiving grubstake interests in the claims.

Ruffner and McKinnon did not have long to wait that winter morning two days later. Douglas and Treadwell soon rode into camp, accompanied by Arthur Whitaker, and the two miners led the visitors up the trail to the claims. For three days Douglas and Treadwell worked in the tunnels and shafts, took samples, examined location papers, and critically inspected contiguous ground, particularly the Azure and Chrome claims, a favorable reference to which was included in his report. At night the visitors slept in McKinnon's tent, while Ruffner rode the five miles to the river to alleviate the loneliness of his wife Sarah, returning each morning.

When the time came for Douglas to leave, he called Ruffner and McKinnon to a conference in the tent. Included was Rod McKinnon, who had arrived in camp.

"First, let me tell you I'm not working for myself," Douglas began, "but for an eastern firm which is interested in mines — when the price is right. If my report should indicate to the partner in this firm who handles mining investments that I consider the Eureka and Wade Hampton good prospects, I must also tell him at what price the claims are offered."

"Twenty-five thousand," Ruffner answered. McKinnon nodded agreement.

Douglas shook his head. "Hundreds of miles from a railroad, rough country — buying them at all is pure speculation. Ten thousand might be considered."

"That wouldn't do," McKinnon declared. "After paying the liens we wouldn't have enough left to make a sale worth while. We've put up our labor for five years, you know."

"Name your rock-bottom price, then."

"We'd have to have at least fifteen."

"Well — I'll see what my principals say. Meantime, I'll risk giving each of you a draft on Philadelphia for five hundred dollars in exchange for options."

The partners agreed. Douglas drafted the option papers, and took the signatures of the miners, which Whitaker and Treadwell witnessed. Then he bade the men good bye and went away, not to return for seven years. When he did come back, it was to inspect the property on behalf of another client.

From Prescott Douglas wired a favorable report to Charles Lennig, of the firm of Logan and Lennig in Philadelphia. The sale went through.

After their debts were settled Ruffner and Angus and Rod McKinnon left the camp with their small fortunes of about thirty-five hundred each. Thus they had relinquished their interest in property which subsequently was to return tens of millions to another owner.

George A. Treadwell, later to attain fame as the developer of the immensely rich Treadwell gold mine in Alaska, liked the looks of the Black Mountain country. He returned to the camp and by advancing money to the locators obtained an interest in some of the claims. He made other locations in the Verde mining district in his own name.

BIG DEAL

Ruffner and his wife sank their money in an irrigation project in the Buckeye country on the Gila. Floods washed out their dam, desert winds drifted sand into their canal, and the project failed. Morris Andrew Ruffner, to whom legend has given the honor of discovering the United Verde mine, died in Phoenix in 1890.

Angus and Rod McKinnon went to Mexico, lured by tales of gold. Let us hope they found it. Their fate appears to be unknown. Their end, like Ruffner's ditch, has been covered by Time's drifting sands.

Jerome three-quarters of a century after its founding.   BERTON F. YOUNG PHOTO

United Verde Smelter, 1883.

New Name in Mining

UNITED VERDE COPPER COMPANY

The year 1882 was a great year for the Verde Valley and for the little mining camp in the Black Mountains. The Atlantic and Pacific railroad, later to be known as the Santa Fe, was pushing steel through north central Arizona, less than fifty miles away. President Chester Arthur had appointed Frederick A. Tritle governor of the Territory of Arizona.

Governor Tritle, being a promoter as well as a politician and a man of means, was busy singing the praises of the territory's resources and the great possibilities which lay in mining, ranching and stockraising. He had come to Prescott in 1880, and one of his earliest excursions was to the Verde Valley in company with William B. Murray, a friend and business associate during his Nevada days, and he and Murray gave financial aid to the hard pressed miners in Black Mountain camp and took as their compensation an interest in some of the claims.

And up and down the valley below pioneers were coming in fast to settle the fertile lands along the river.

Word of the richness of the Verde mineral deposits was spreading. In the fall of the year a man arrived in the camp from Nevada, by the name of F. F. Thomas, well known to Tritle and Murray. The three men evolved a plan to consolidate the better claims under an incorporated company and undertake development. Thomas was a mining engineer with a degree from the Yale School of Mines, with twenty years of practical experience, and well qualified to direct the undertaking in mind.

Financed by Tritle and Murray, Thomas obtained options on the claims contiguous to the Eureka and Wade Hampton and two claims with fine mineral showings which lay a couple of miles southward — the Ventures North and South. Then the engineer hurried east, armed with letters of introduction from his partners. The letter from Murray was addressed to Eugene M. Jerome of New York, a prominent young attorney who had requested his cousin William B. Murray to keep an eye open for a good investment in mining.

Thomas first visited Charles Lennig in Philadelphia, and found him not averse to joining a development enterprise with the Eureka and Wade Hampton to be included in a consolidation. Lennig gave him a letter of introduction to James A. Macdonald, an insurance executive, who was also interested in mining investments.

In New York Thomas's glowing account of the richness of the Arizona mines aroused the keen interest of Macdonald and Jerome, who lent their aid in the formation of a corporation. A capitalist by the name of Bushnell agreed to join in the financing.

Early in 1883 the United Verde Copper Company became a New York corporation with Macdonald as president, Tritle as vice president, and Jerome as secretary. In addition to these three officers Tritle, Bushnell and Lennig were made members of the board of directors. The company was capitalized for $3,000,000, and the issuance of 300,000 shares at a par value of $10 each was authorized.

Thomas was employed as superintendent of the mines, and with $200,000 pledged, mostly from the directors, he was instructed to take up the options and start operations.

In consideration for his placing the Eureka and Wade Hampton in the enterprise, Lennig was issued $75,000 in first lien mortgage bonds.

When the purchase of the claims had been completed at a cost of $90,000, the company had in its possession eleven claims and two millsites.

Thomas's first endeavor in the development program was to provide avenues of transportation. Some help was received from Yavapai County, but by the time a wagon road was built to Fort Verde to connect with the military road to Prescott, and another across the rugged hills to connect with the Prescott–Ash Fork wagon road to rail, the treasury had been further depleted by $25,000. Next a thirty-six inch water jacket blast furnace with a capacity of 40 tons of ore a day was shipped from Chicago and freighted in by mule team from Ash Fork, together with a rock crusher and blower, and steam engines to operate the blower and a hoist for a double compartment shaft on the Wade Hampton claim where the first ores were to be mined.

The problem of water supply was solved by building a pipe line to a spring two miles away. Coke was shipped from New Mexico, later to be supplemented by a better grade from Wales via the west coast after the completion of the railroad to tidewater. An office building was constructed, together with other buildings which included an assay office, blacksmith shop, and dormitory and boarding house. These were all wooden structures, the lumber being supplied from a sawmill on the pine grown mountain. The little furnace was erected, and smelting was ready to begin.

The blowing-in was done on August 1, 1883. Employed at the mine and smelter were seventy-five men, mostly Irish, as old Erin was still the fountainhead for a substantial portion of the labor employed in the United States. A payroll of the period showed only one name of Spanish origin, though in later years there came a flood of workmen from Mexico.

On that payroll was the name of a man who rates a story of his own — Frederick Everest Murray, brother of William B., a cousin of Eugene Jerome. Murray was actually serving as watchdog for Eugene, though he was rated as a furnace tapper at a wage of four dollars a day.

Downtown building was proceeding rapidly. A townsite was laid out and surface rights sold to mining claims. Lumber from the sawmill supplemented the extensive use of poles and canvas. From the slopes rough streets were gouged which in rainy season became muddy bogs. A saloon was opened, to be followed by another, and a grocery store with clothing and hardware as side lines. Women came, first the ladies who gave the unattached miners company and pleasure, then the wives of the married men. More claims were located in the mountains around the town. A post office was established with F. F. Thomas the first postmaster.

To the joy of the promoters, the ore appeared to be plentiful and in no danger of exhaustion. Every extension of tunnels and shafts was in ore, most of it rich. It averaged twenty to thirty percent copper near the surface, with high values in silver and gold.

It was hot in the furnace shed that day in August, but no one complained. As the first matte was drawn, Superintendent Thomas felt that he had reached the most satisfying point in his life. When the first bar of the black copper was knocked from the mould, he looked upon it as a beautiful thing. He would have liked to keep it as a souvenir of a dream come true, but with its high gold and silver content it was too valuable to let lie around. It went away with the first wagon train loaded with bars for shipment to the refinery from Ash Fork.

All was not to be clear sailing. In the days which followed there were numerous hampering delays. In the five remaining months of 1883 the furnace was down thirty-four days because of rains and mishaps which prevented the delivery of coke and other supplies. Yet in that period two million pounds of copper were produced, together with 125,000 ounces of silver and a pleasing amount of gold which would be separated from the copper in the refining process.

Mining during the first months of operation was comparatively easy. The steep hillside made the tunneling method of ore extraction simple, and the cost of sinking in the still shallow shafts was not excessive. The ores, largely oxide, were the richest the mine was ever to encounter. But as the tunnels were extended farther and the shafts sunk deeper heavy timbering and longer hauls and hoisting became necessary, with ever increasing costs. Worse, the ores became leaner as mining progressed, while the sulphur content increased, making it necessary to pile and roast the ores before sending them to the furnace.

The financial panic which struck New York in May 1884 depressed the metal market; by fall copper prices had suffered a drastic decline. Freight costs from smelter to refinery were more than $70.00 a ton. Though still very rich by the standard of later day mines, the United Verde could not then produce copper under the existing primitive conditions at a cost which would yield a profit.

In October 1884 the smelter and mines were closed following a strike by the workmen because the payment of their wages was delayed. The United Verde Copper Company under its original management was to produce no more metal.

Yet the little plant's record had been impressive, a tribute to Superintendent Thomas's training and skill, combined with superhuman effort. On Jerome's Main Street today there is on display the rusted shell of the little furnace he operated. It is rather hard to imagine that from so small a piece of equipment, during a running time totalling not more than 300 days, it poured from its fiery bowl more than 4,000,000 pounds of copper, which contained what now would seem the astonishing amount of 235,000 ounces of silver. With the gold content the total value of metals produced was close to $800,000.

The closing of the smelter was a gloomy day for little Jerome, and to many it seemed that it should not have been necessary. It had made money. The first returns from the refinery had caused jubilation among the directors, and raised their hopes high. Their investment appeared to be secure. As large profits were no doubt to continue, why build up bank accounts? Dividends were in order, and the directors happily voted them to the extent the treasury would allow. By August 1, 1884, the United

Verde had distributed $97,500, not anticipating nor providing for such a contingency as the fatal drop in copper which forced the closing of the operation. In consequence the company was left with a depleted treasury to provide for maintenance and other expenses during the coming years — a period so depressing that the directors would seek to sell the property three years later.

In retrospect, what seemed so fine a production for the brief period the little smelter was in operation under Thomas's supervision appears small indeed in comparison with the production of the United Verde mine under subsequent ownership. Though the essential purpose of this narrative is to tell of the people and events of the early days, let us here inject this epilogue: By the time the United Verde mine had been worked out in 1953 it had produced two and a half billion pounds of copper, fifty million ounces of silver, a million ounces of gold, and many millions of pounds of zinc, with a gross value in excess of half a billion dollars.

Yet this mine, while the largest and richest, was but one of several producers in the mountains around Jerome.

The rusty bowl of the little blast furnace which in 1883 and 1884, more than eighty years ago, smelted four million pounds of copper.

Eugene Murray Jerome

The Man from Williamstown
EUGENE MURRAY JEROME

Eugene Jerome was bone tired. He had lost too much sleep over this damned Arizona mine. As dusk dimmed his office in Temple Court, Beekman Street, New York City, he stored the uncompleted briefs, conveyances and estate papers in the safe, snapped on a light, and returned to his desk.

He sat down and drew a pile of United Verde papers toward him. He hated to dig into it. There were too many bills.

Something would have to give soon. He had hoped for a break when Fred Tritle had leased the mine and smelter at the Verde the previous summer, but that hope had gone glimmering. Tritle had gone broke, and now both he and Lennig were pressing Jerome, Macdonald and Bushnell, who had been appointed to act as trustees in winding up the company's affairs.

There was hope that a sale could be made. James Douglas, representing the Copper Queen interests of Phelps, Dodge and Company had recently visited the mines a second time and was now in New York to discuss acquisition of the United Verde. Fred Murray, already in town, was enjoying the bright lights while waiting for the conference, set for tomorrow. Tritle was also on hand and Lennig stood ready to come up from Philadelphia if the conference produced results.

Eugene felt irritation every time he thought of Tritle. Even though the former Arizona governor was a stockholder and a member of the board of directors, he had been too arrogant and insistent upon having his own way; he had been a critic of the company's administration ever since the beginning of the enterprise, and had fought against and become very bitter over the cancellation of his lease. Lennig too was critical, with more cause, and if a sale could not be made it was probable he would foreclose.

It had been a tough grind during the past three years, since the drastic decline in the price of copper had caught the officials unaware. They would simply have to make a sale, and Fred Murray seemed confident that one could be negotiated, if not with Douglas then with someone else.

Jerome's cousin Fred Murray, who had been put in charge of the properties after the shutdown, had also been a cause for worry. Though he was intelligent and likeable, his addiction to liquor and the pursuit of enjoyment, and his too frequent trips to Prescott on "business" which could have just as well been conducted by mail, had resulted in the property not having been maintained as well as it should have been.

Eugene was fond of his handsome cousin, even though compelled to criticize his actions. Many an evening he had worked into the night writing long letters to Murray in his neat and flowing script, urging him to get on the ball and let liquor alone and reminding him of the substantial financial returns he might expect when the property resumed operations or was sold. He knew Murray resented this, even though he showed restraint in his reactions. Since he had arrived for the conference with Douglas and his associates he had been cheerful; strangely so, Eugene felt, for he himself didn't have too much faith in the possibility of a deal, especially with the hampering influence of Tritle and Lennig. Yet Fred just smiled at such expressions of doubt, and said that if the Copper Queen didn't want the United Verde, someone else would. Jerome presumed Murray referred to W. A. Clark, the young Montana millionaire. Jerome didn't think much of that prospect, for he had sounded out Clark himself and had found him vague as to his interest in the mine. He had seemed more interested in a contemplated trip to Paris.

On this particular evening in January, 1888, Eugene checked the list of liabilities he always kept at his elbow, and added some more from the demands recently received. It wasn't a very pretty picture. The commitments added up to a little better than $30,000 in addition to the Lennig bonds.

Jerome finally slammed shut his roll top desk and went home. Perhaps tomorrow he would know whether or not he could resume a normal life and concentrate on his law practice.

But tomorrow didn't produce definite results. Jerome met with Murray and Douglas, but got no further than a general discussion on terms which early produced disagreement. Douglas was a hard bargainer. For a week they wrestled with the problem of adjusting their differences. On January 12 they reached a tentative plan to present to the directors. For his principals Douglas proposed to advance $30,000 to pay off the indebtedness; they would take the property under lease and bond and spend up to $200,000 in development. For each pound of copper produced they would return a percentage to the stockholders.

The United Verde representatives finally agreed to the proposal, subject to shareholders' approval. Jerome agreed to begin drafting the necessary papers the next day and to notify the other directors and stockholders of the plan.

Jerome's fear that Lennig and Tritle might throw a monkey wrench into the machinery of negotiation proved justified. Lennig arrived in New York on January 16 and dissented. Tritle went along with him, for some quick money was what both wanted.

Lennig proposed an alternate plan, which called for the Phelps Dodge and Company interests buying the outstanding shares at a dollar each and absorption of the debts. Refusing to deal on any other basis, Lennig returned to Philadelphia.

Douglas and his lawyer would not agree to the Lennig proposal unless the provision regarding assuming the debts was eliminated. Lennig stood firm. All indications were that the deal had blown up. On January 30 Douglas finally agreed to negotiate on Lennig's terms, but found he was too late.

While Clark remained in the background, other possible purchasers had entered the picture. Tom Bullock, who under a territorial subsidy had built a railroad from Seligman on the Atlantic and Pacific to Prescott, began negotiations for a lease, claiming he could raise the needed capital. He furnished no proof that he could, and he passed out of the picture. Then F. F. Thomas brought in a man named Lawler who was interested in purchasing the United Verde, on terms which the trustees rejected. Brief negotiations were held with a Boston firm, representing French capital, but it was apparent they were looking for a bargain on bankrupt terms.

Then, on February 14, Murray asked for a meeting of the trustees to talk with William A. Clark, who Murray said had just returned from Paris. The trustees, while knowing of Clark's interest in the United Verde, had not taken seriously the possibility of his meeting their terms, knowing his reputation for obtaining properties on a liquidation basis. They told Clark of the terms laid down by Lennig, and received a surprise.

"I'll negotiate on that basis," Clark told them. He would take a lease and option on the property, retire all debts, and buy in the stockholders' shares.

Two days later the agreement was signed. "OK. Whoops!" Murray wrote in his diary. He and Jerome went up to the Union Club and celebrated.

On February 21 the deal was approved at a meeting of the stockholders. William Andrews Clark was on his way to riches beyond his dreams, Eugene Jerome to peace of mind and an easier life, and Fred Murray to oblivion.

During the years of his venture into mining Eugene Murray Jerome was the best known member of the well-known Murray and Jerome families of Canandagua and Syracuse, New York. His cousin William Travers Jerome, also a rising young attorney, was in later years to attain international prominence as the public prosecutor in the notorious Harry Thaw–Stanford White murder case.

Eugene was a man of unusually attractive and charming personality. He was a descendent of families prominent since colonial days, some with revolutionary war records. A Seneca Indian chief, according to family tradition, was among the Jeromes' ancestors. A son of Addison Gardiner Jerome and Julia Gould Jerome, he was born in Syracuse in 1845 and graduated from Williams College in the class of 1867, and shortly thereafter was married to Paulina von Schneidau of Chicago. He was a nephew of Leonard Jerome, the father of Jennie, who was to become Lady Randolph Churchill and the mother of Sir Winston.

Eugene Jerome studied law in New York and for many years maintained an office in that city. With a profitable law practice, a comfortable inheritance and an adventurous spirit, he had enthusiastically entered the United Verde promotion and exerted a tremendous amount of time and energy in directing its affairs.

He worked prodigiously, even to the detriment of his health, to keep the company from dissolution during the dreary days of the depression when the treasury was empty.

Upon his retirement from his law practice Eugene Jerome returned to his home in Williamstown, Massachusetts, where he died on February 14, 1914.

Eugene Jerome's Town, 1883.

Eugene Jerome's Town, 1963. Cleaning up debris of some of the town's vanished business buildings.

FREDERICK E. MURRAY

The Man from Canandagua

FREDERICK EVEREST MURRAY

As he tramped wearily up to the mine boarding house where he bunked, Fred Murray felt his hatred of the little mining camp grow. He had spent that day in the late fall of 1887 shoring up timbers in the Eureka tunnel, with only one helper, and he was tired and dirty.

What a hell of a way to live. In name he was agent for the United Verde Company, and physical labor was degrading. The only thing that kept him going was the prospect that a sale of the properties was under consideration, according to Eugene Jerome, and he was due to benefit through his stock holdings.

Fred Murray hated the camp for several reasons. He came from an aristocratic family, whose members considered it altogether fitting that a cousin on the Jerome side should have become the wife of an English lord. He hated the isolation, for he loved bright lights and gaiety and the company of the women which went with them. He hated the primitive conditions under which he was forced to live, the coarse food, and the board shack which was his home. He hated the eternal probing of Eugene Jerome into his personal life, and the criticism of almost every act performed on his own initiative.

He undressed, hung his mucked-up work attire on a nail, bathed from a tin wash basin, and carefully brushed his hair and beard. After putting on clean clothing he prepared his supper. He was glad for the quail Charley Willard had sent up from the valley — they were good even though he had cooked them a little too well.

After eating he strolled downtown to get a bottle of something that would help him forget his irritations. He considered joining a listless poker game in the saloon, but discarded the idea when he learned that there was a two-bit limit. The miners and merchants left in the town after Tritle's fiasco earlier in the year were mostly broke.

On his way back up the hill he almost stepped on a rattlesnake, and chilled to think what a ghastly end the reptile might have brought him.

41

He smashed its head with a rock and kicked it over the edge of the road.

It had been a warm day, and he opened the door and windows of his quarters to let the room cool. For awhile he sat outside, watching a full moon rise over the Mogollon rim. It made him think of romances unattainable in this God-forsaken spot, and he went inside. When he lit his kerosene lamp and glanced up at the wall clock to learn the time, he saw a big hairy tarantula on the clock's face. Cursing, he disposed of it. The odor of a skunk permeated the room; he should not have shot the varmint while it was under the house the day before.

He undressed, and after carefully inspecting his bunk to see that no centipedes or scorpions had taken refuge there he crawled into bed. With the lamp close to his pillow he read a few pages of "The Tinted Venus", but his restlessness prevented concentration. He laid the book aside, took a generous swallow from his bottle, and blew out the light. The mourning of a coyote down the gulch added to his sense of loneliness.

Sleep was slow in coming. He brooded over the anomalous position he held. "One fourth lackey, one fourth boss, and one half sucker," he had described himself. Eugene didn't trust him much. He recalled bitterly certain letters he had received from his cousin.

"You have been foolish indeed," one complained, "yet with the prospect of a fortune coming to you some day you should get yourself in shape to use it. You are too good a fellow to throw yourself away on rum."

In another letter he had been even more pontifical:

"I am sending you a formal appointment (as agent) and I must depend on you hereafter for good faith. You will recognize the fact that in relying on you as sole representative of my forty thousand dollars, as well as your expected sixty thousand, I am going to the front pretty strong for you. Now, my dear fellow, be cautious and dignified, but firm. Swallow all the crow you can for peace. Permit no rum in the company's office or lounge with bummers. Show good executive ability now and give me the opportunity to advance you . . ."

Fred gritted his teeth. Eat crow, indeed. Eugene seemed to have overlooked the fact that he had actually saved the company from disaster by staving off impatient creditors who had been ready to serve attachments. Just one vital service out of many. If Eugene could have seen him at such times, smiling and suave while seething inside, he would respect him more and criticize less.

What, Fred asked himself, would Eugene have done if torn away from everything he cherished and planted on a wilderness mountain side, harassed by snakes and vermin, drenching summer rains and winter snows, as well as creditors? He had tried to get Jerome to visit the mines and see for himself the degrading conditions under which he was forced to live, but the New Yorker claimed to be too busy staving off debtors at his end and raising money for the mine's maintenance. Eugene was soft, that was what.

Well, deliverance shouldn't be too far off. Hope of reviving the mining and smelting operation was diminishing day by day. The United Verde would have to be sold. Two or three deals were on the fire. One of which Fred was hopeful Eugene Jerome didn't know about yet — he had had some correspondence with William A. Clark, and felt sure that if he should become the owner of the mines he would have a place for Fred. Clark was a man to cultivate.

Tomorrow, Fred decided as he went to sleep, he would send word to have his horse Billy brought up from George Hull's ranch, where it was in pasture. He would spend the weekend in Prescott and forget his troubles for a little while.

The Murrays were of an old and well-known family of New York state, descendants of Reuben Murray of revolutionary days. Frederick was born in Canandagua in 1849. His father was an anti-slavery whig, and a Lincoln appointee to the postmastership of Canandagua. He continued in that office until his retirement because of illness the year before his death in 1879.

Fred had three brothers; one, Albert, a graduate of West Point, had been an officer in the Union army and died a prisoner of war in Georgia. Henry, another brother, served in the Civil War, and the third, William B., was successful in mining in Nevada, New Mexico and Arizona, and died in New Mexico not long after he had assisted in the organization of the United Verde.

Fred attended Yale, but did not graduate. At the college he was known as an artist of some promise, a linguist, and a writer who had several articles accepted for publication by well known magazines.

Then as always he had been plagued by a shortage of funds. He tried writing as a vocation after leaving college, and sold several short stories, but the income was insignificant as compared to his needs. He tried reading law, but gave it up as too demanding of his time. After the death of his father and the obligation of helping support his mother arose, he had asked Eugene Jerome to use his influence in securing for him a position worthy of his talents. Eugene sent him to Arizona as his watchdog at the newly organized United Verde Copper Company. Fred was warned by his cousin that he would have to work, but promised to have a substantial block of shares in the company set aside to be paid for out of his inheritance when his brother William's estate was settled.

Fred Murray had poise, charm when he elected to turn it on, versatility of speech and a love of good clothes. With a patrician nose, broad forehead, a fine moustache twisted upward at the ends, and a short beard swept to either side in a social style of the day, he was a striking figure of a man. In Arizona he went Western to the extent that he liked to appear in a wide brimmed, flat crowned white Stetson, jacket and vest of soft leather, and a colorful stock. Thus he appeared when on weekends he saddled his horse and took the trail through Lonesome Valley to Prescott, to cajole the merchants, smile at the ladies, and spend Saturday and Sunday evenings at the gay bars of Montezuma Street — the famous Whiskey Row.

It was a happy day for Fred Murray when in mid-December of 1887 he received a telegram from Eugene Jerome to come on to New York, as matters seemed to have progressed to the point of negotiation with James Douglas. He enjoyed to the full the Christmas holidays in the metropolis. Douglas was there, and Murray had talks with him, during which Douglas informed him that if the deal for the purchase of the United Verde went through he would be offered the position of superintendent. This was confirmation, Fred thought, of his foresight in striving to make a favorable impression on the Professor. This was a more positive offer than Clark had indicated.

As Arizona agent of the United Verde, together with a quality of charm that matched Eugene Jerome's, Murray sat in on all negotiations with Douglas and his attorney during January. When at the end of the month the parties failed to reach an agreement Murray hastened to get in touch with Clark, and the troubles of the United Verde were over so far as the immediate financial needs were concerned.

Clark returned Murray to Jerome as his agent, a position he held until the new lessee's own technicians took over in May. He then represented the interests of Jerome and his associates until Clark took up his lease and option in January 1890 and became the owner of ninety-five percent of the shares of the company.

THE MAN FROM CANANDAGUA

In appreciation of the work Murray had done in getting them off the hook, Jerome persuaded the directors to vote Fred a two thousand dollar bonus. After the death of his mother he became heir to her estate. He did some scouting of mining claims for James Douglas.

From this time on Frederick Murray's life is obscure. It is certain that within a few years his money was gone. His own relatives never learned when and where he died. The last word of Frederick Murray we have had came through James S. Douglas, son of the Professor and developer of the United Verde Extension mine. On different occasions, he said, he had heard his father speak of Murray.

One day in the late nineties Professor Douglas met Murray on a street in downtown New York. He was not the natty, assured man of earlier years. He showed the effects of dissipation. His clothes were shabby, his beard was unkempt, and he was hollow-eyed. But at sight of Douglas he straightened up and tried to appear at ease.

"Why, Professor!" he exclaimed. "I'm happy to see you again!"

They shook hands, and Douglas inquired as to Murray's activities.

"I'm writing a book on life in a mining camp," Murray answered. "Also, I've been writing articles and stories for various publications." He paused. "But — right now I find myself in an embarrassing situation — publishers are notoriously slow in payment. Drafts I have been expecting have failed to arrive. I wonder —" He paused again; he tried to smile, but his lips had a bitter twist. "I'm wondering if you could make me a small loan to tide me over — just temporary, of course."

"Of course." That the debonair Fred Murray should have descended to panhandling was shocking, but with the shock came a feeling of pity.

There was evidently further delay in the arrival of the drafts, for the touch was repeated on subsequent occasions. Once Douglas asked Murray why he didn't get Eugene Jerome to give him assistance. Murray laughed.

"Dear old Cousin Gene," he said. "So fatherly, so persistent an advisor. Such warmth of heart, such brotherly love! I've urged him to don the cloth."

Those who knew Fred Murray's story could only feel regret that this handsome and gifted man, a member of a respected line of American pioneers and one who had a part in the making of millionaires, should have become estranged from family and friends, should have descended to destitution and possible degradation, and should have been buried in an unknown grave, perhaps in a potter's field.

FREDERICK A. TRITLE

The Man from Pennsylvania

FREDERICK AUGUSTUS TRITLE

Frederick Tritle, once governor of the Territory of Arizona, tossed aside the copy of the Prescott Courier he had been reading. An Article on the United Verde Copper Company under William A. Clark's management, and the wealth pouring from the smelter at Jerome, depressed him.

He arose from his chair and moved to the fire place in the living room of his Prescott home. On the mantle was a small bar of black copper, which he had cast in a special mold from the first pour from the little old smelter after he had leased the property in 1887. He fingered it gloomily.

Tritle's son Harry came into the room.

"Let's quit looking backward, Dad," he said. "I know you're thinking that piece of blister is probably the most expensive piece of unfabricated copper in the world — it cost you three hundred and fifty thousand dollars. But let's stop mourning about it. We're getting along all right."

Falteringly, for he had been ill, Frederick Tritle returned to his chair. Watching the flame in the fireplace he let his thoughts wander back to earlier and happier days; back to the fields and forests of his native Pennsylvania; to California, where he had found and married the charming woman who had been at his side for forty years; then to Nevada, where he had become a man of influence and wealth; and finally to the few short years when, as governor of the young Territory of Arizona, an energetic administration had brought him acclaim throughout the Southwest.

Frederick Augustus Tritle was born at Chambersburg, Pennsylvania, in 1833, of Holland Dutch stock. He studied law, but practiced only briefly in his home state before harkening to the call of the West. By way of Iowa he reached California in 1859, where at Sacramento he met and married the lovely Jane Katherine Hereford, whose father had practiced law with Abraham Lincoln, and one of whose brothers was a United States senator from West Virginia.

Newly discovered bonanza mines in Nevada were luring thousands to that vigorous young territory. Tritle caught the fever, and he and his bride moved to Carson City, where he opened a law office, specializing in mining law. From law he branched out into the business and political fields. He accepted the management of a store; he helped organize Ormsby County, and was elected one of its first commissioners.

He became active in the development of mines, and moved to Virginia City. He became president of two mines and a director of a railroad. He was a shrewd investor, and accumulated a fortune of more than a quarter of a million dollars — small fare in comparison with the multimillions of Mackay and Sharon and Fair, but enough to allow him time to enjoy his flair for politics. In 1865 he was elected state senator from Storey County, then he raised his sights. His final goal was Washington.

He was a handsome man, suave and polished, well educated and distinguished of appearance. He wore a flowing beard, and was of the "long-head" type, believed to indicate superior intelligence. He was a good orator, his style fluent and pleasing.

In 1864 Nevada had been made a state. Tritle decided to test his political charisma by a try for the governorship. In 1870 he opposed, as a Republican, L. R. Bradley who was seeking reelection on the Democratic ticket. Tritle lost.

For the next ten years he devoted himself to making money and extending his acquaintance throughout the state. In 1880 he became a candidate for United States senator.

Though comparisons were hard to make in an era riddled with political corruption, even many of Nevada's own citizens claimed their state had the most corrupt government of any state in the nation. Perhaps that brand was applied because the politicians with the money sacks operated more openly than those in the older states. Vast fortunes had been made, and with them came the urge for political control, in some cases for political office. Tritle did not have a great fortune to spend on buying votes; nevertheless his good friend Senator John P. Jones urged him to make the race.

He had millions in wealth against him. Senator William Sharon, who had entered the state with a fortune made in California, and whose term was expiring, was expected to seek reelection. Sharon was condemned statewide as one who had neglected Nevada's interests — one who, as General Grant was quoted as saying, "lives in California, votes in Nevada, and carries the state in his vest pocket." Another accusation was that "he bought legislators as openly as he bought mining stocks."

Tritle had wide support from the Nevada press, including a substantial portion of the Democratic newspapers, which loudly proclaimed that Sharon's only hope was to buy the needed votes in the legislature, which then elected the senators. Sharon was ready, it was claimed, to spend two or three hundred thousand dollars for these purchases, more if required. Nevertheless Tritle's election was widely predicted.

Then another opponent came charging into the picture. Colonel James G. Fair, of Bonanza fame, sought the office. Worth forty-two million dollars, he was prepared to cut that fortune down to an even forty million, so his enemies declared, if he could buy the senatorial toga.

What happened then has never been clear. Tritle withdrew, and why he did so was the cause of many rumors. He had become ill; he had been bought off; he was hoping for a presidential appointment. The truth probably rests in the fact that Tritle simply did not have the money to compete with the bulging sacks of the multimillionaires, and real money it would take.

In any case, Tritle left Nevada for California with his wife and five children, to recuperate, according to press reports.

Senator Sharon returned to private life. Colonel Fair went to Washington, where he soon gained national notoriety as "Nevada's Wicked Senator." He established a "seraglio", according to newspaper accounts, only to have it raided by his strong-willed wife, who then left him. Fair also warred with his son, who tried to shoot him. Tritle took grim satisfaction in pasting in his scrap books the newspaper accounts of such escapades.

Senator Jones then proposed that Tritle place himself in a position to gain appointment as governor of Arizona Territory from James A. Garfield, the new president. John C. Frémont, the noted general, explorer and politician, was then Arizona's governor, appointed by President Hayes as a tribute to his service to the country after he had lost his fortune in disastrous California ventures. Frémont was under attack by Arizona newspapers, who claimed that he treated the office of governor as a sinecure, and was absent from the territory most of the time. Too, he was getting old.

In Nevada Tritle had been associated with William B. Murray in mining ventures, and they had become friends. Murray encouraged Tritle to settle in Arizona, and he left for Prescott. He immediately identified himself with Arizona's interests, and acquired wide acquaintance and popularity, in which a strong factor was the support of his charming and talented wife.

At Murray's suggestion Tritle investigated the Black Mountains claims and acquired an interest in some of them by the route of grubstaking.

When Chester A. Arthur became President following Garfield's assassination, Senator Jones recommended him again for the office of governor of Arizona Territory. In this he was supported by other influential senators and by members of Jane Tritle's family.

Tritle was appointed and took office in February 1882. He had been a resident of Arizona for a year and a half; a factor influencing his appointment was the wide support he had gained from prominent citizens of Arizona, who had been pleased with the obvious interest he had shown in the affairs of the Territory and who thought it time a real resident of Arizona be their governor.

Tritle traveled widely through the territory, which then had a population of 60,000, and visited all the important communities, and institutions. He worked for the development of schools, mines, agriculture and stockraising. He investigated the activities of the "Indian Ring" at the San Carlos reservation, where corrupt officials were issuing passes to Indians to leave the reservation, then appropriating money and supplies which should have gone to their support. Many of the Indians released joined marauding bands. Tritle vowed to break the ring.

He was appalled at the ineffective action against the Indians still on the warpath, and at the lawlessness at Tombstone, which he visited and reported seven murders in the seven days he was there. He assisted in organizing companies of militia to aid in suppressing lawlessness among both the Indians and the white bandits and rustlers, financing to be done in part by citizens and in part by loans backed by promises of appropriations from the legislature.

Tritle made a trip to Washington, and took a strong stand with the President and Secretary of War Robert T. Lincoln in soliciting aid to subdue the Indians and the white criminals. He succeeded in persuading the President to issue a proclamation condemning the lawlessness in Cochise County and calling upon all good citizens to help subdue it. He demanded that Secretary Lincoln return General Crook to Arizona from the Department of the Platte; this at first met with refusal, but Lincoln finally gave in.

Tritle was condemned by opposition newspapers, and by law enforcement officers and some influential citizens of Tombstone for interfering in the Cochise County situation. But he persisted. The war between the deputy marshals Earp and Sheriff Behan of Cochise County was raging. When the Earps and Doc Holliday fled to Colorado after they killed a man at Tucson in Pima County, the governor refused to give Behan a request for extradition for the so-called criminals, but did give a petition to Sheriff Paul of Pima County. Defiantly Behan went to Denver and tried to bluff the authorities there to surrender the Earps. The bluff failed.

Tritle continued his connection with mines in Yavapai County, even though the opposition press condemned him for it. He had a hand in the incorporation of the United Verde Copper Company in 1883 and was named vice-president not so much for the reason that he owned an interest in the claims as for the prestige his official position conveyed. Eugene Jerome soon regretted this, as Tritle became an irritant because of his constant insistence that he be given an active voice in the company's management and his criticism of the manner in which its business was handled.

In 1884 the Democratic party elected Grover Cleveland President, their first successful candidate since James Buchanan. In October 1885 Tritle was replaced as governor by Conrad M. Zulick, but he was now a confirmed Arizonan and remained in Prescott.

After the United Verde's little furnace and the mines were closed in the fall of 1884, Tritle chafed at the idleness of the property and began to dream of acquiring it for himself. With copper prices beginning to advance he negotiated a lease in July, 1887, and set about restoring the mines to production. He hired labor gangs and with some aid from the county restored the road to Prescott. A shorter route to rail was now available as the Prescott and Arizona Central Railway from Seligman on the Atlantic and Pacific had reached Prescott. In this preparatory work Tritle expended twenty-five thousand dollars.

He then erected the second furnace which had been acquired just prior to the time the original smelter run had ended; he restored the shafts and drifts and renovated the mechanical equipment. Then he began to produce copper, with errors and delays due to the lack of properly trained aides.

Returns from the metal produced were slow in coming in and disappointing when they did come. Mining was much more expensive than anticipated; the ores were growing leaner in content and running to sulphides, requiring the extra step of roasting. There were expensive delays caused by breakdowns of equipment.

Tritle's cash was gone; he had borrowed all he could. The workmen rioted because their wages were overdue. Only two thousand dollars of the ten thousand owed the United Verde as first payment on the lease had been paid. Eugene Jerome was not disposed to leniency and directed Fred Murray to serve notice of cancellation. Tritle was deeply resentful, but he had no alternative to closing the operation after a run of about a month.

Late in the year Tritle traveled to New York in an attempt to speed up settlement for metal shipped to the Orford Refinery and to urge sale of the United Verde. He tried to raise money on his stock, but found no buyers for shares in an enterprise which could not show a profit.

"Tritle has seen me several times since his arrival," Jerome wrote Murray in November, "and I am surprised to find him so broken, both mentally and physically. It seems that his necessities are very great. . . . Of course, he is bitter against you and thinks his downfall due mainly to you and your 'gab'."

Tritle blamed Murray, as agent for the United Verde, for interference in the operation of his lease and for unfavorable reports regarding his management.

After his participation in the sale of the United Verde to William A. Clark, Tritle returned to Prescott. After liquidating his debts, or as many of them as he could, he found himself a very poor man. He held minor political offices and from 1894 through 1897 he was recorder for Yavapai County.

Though the substance of the incident related in the opening paragraphs of this chapter was told to me by the late Charles W. Fairfield, a former state auditor and a close friend of Harry Tritle, it is doubtful that Frederick Tritle could have dropped such a large sum in the United Verde alone. In a letter to Fred Murray Eugene Jerome said Tritle's losses on his lease exceeded sixty thousand dollars, and with the sale of the United Verde to Clark he probably recovered his investment in the shares of the corporation. He appears to have lost a great deal of money in operations connected with his acquirement of mines and interests in the mines of the area which did not become producers. His original fortune was acquired through speculation in mines. He tried to repeat, and failed.

It is probable that the mine in the Black Mountains was considered by Tritle's family as the main villain in a series of operations, and was used as the symbol of disaster. Yet because of the United Verde's subsequent fame Tritle's connection with it will not be forgotten.

Frederick Augustus Tritle died in Phoenix in 1906. History should record that he was one of the most active, successful and popular governors of Arizona's territorial days.

United Verde Miners. (Jerome Historical Society, Matheus Col.)

WILLIAM A. CLARK

The Man from Montana

WILLIAM ANDREWS CLARK

It can be saddening to see vigor regress to frailty, energy to enervation. That was my thought when Senator Clark made his last trip to Clarkdale in 1924. Within that year the eighty-five year old millionaire had shown increasing sign of uncertainty in movement and thought.

He had come slowly down the stairway from his richly draped and mahogany furnished offices on the second floor of the Clarkdale general office building, on the way to join his son Charles and general manager Robert E. Tally for a stroll in the smelter yards. Not through the vast smelter as always before, I knew, as I had heard the decision made that the Senator must be dissuaded from undergoing the physical activity required to make his usual tour of inspection.

The entrance to my office was near the exit door. The Senator stepped in, held out his hand and greeted me cordially.

"I'm glad to see you again," he said. "And how is your family?"

I told him my family was fine.

He went out the door. He and those awaiting him entered a car and drove the few hundred feet to the corridor which led to the roaring furnaces and converters. They got out, strolled about a bit, and seemed to be engaged in an argument. After a quarter of an hour the three re-entered the car and rolled back to the office. The Senator alighted, brushing off an offer of assistance, and turned back into the building. He looked in through my open door, turned and entered. He held out his hand and greeted me cordially.

"I'm glad to see you again," he said. "And how is your family?"

I told him my family was fine.

The reins which Senator Clark had held so firmly and so long were about to pass to other hands.

The man who for thirty-seven years directed the destinies of the United Verde Copper Company, and through it the towns of Jerome and Clarkdale, was a small man physically but dominant in personality. He could be

55

friendly or ruthless, kind to his employees or a fierce antagonist of his enemies. He could squeeze a dollar or spend a million according to the purpose to be accomplished.

Though short of stature, the appearance of William A. Clark was striking. He wore a mop of red hair, carefully tended in apparently careless style. Beneath a hawk-like nose lay his heavy upswept moustache, partially concealing a thin lipped mouth that some called firm, others cruel. His beard was parted and swept to either side — one writer described it as "the beard of a minor prophet." Even in his old age the Senator's hair and beard retained their reddish appearance, though through them streaks of pale sorrel showed the bleaching process of the years.

His piercing eyes might bring chills, and often did. They had never been known to cringe. Why should they ever, when back of them was a brain seething with confidence and pride bred by the power born of high success?

Thus the Senator, as after the turn of the century he was universally known, had equipment to compensate for his lack of height. No one who ever had contact with him could forget him. His movements were quick and forceful. His dress was that of his period's idea of a successful and dominant man. Seldom was he seen without a swallow tail coat. When afoot on his business sallies he didn't walk — he strode; he would match the progress of a taller companion step for step. Watching his energetic advance one might receive the impression that he was preparing to break into a lope.

In his palatial private railroad car, said to be the last to be used as he used it in America — to transport the person and entourage of a king — he traveled often between New York, Chicago, Butte, Salt Lake City, Los Angeles and Jerome Junction, and later Clarkdale — or wherever his extensive business interest called him — accompanied by secretary and servants. It was a glad day for him when he first traveled over the rails of his own San Pedro, Los Angeles and Salt Lake line, built at vast expense from United Verde profits, he boasted, in a race with a competing line being pushed by the Union Pacific to the Southern California Coast.

Until a broad-gauge rail line was built by the Santa Fe into Clarkdale in 1912, for which the Senator advanced the cost, he would leave his car at Jerome Junction on the Ash Fork–Phoenix branch of the Santa Fe and complete his journey to Jerome over his narrow gauge United Verde & Pacific in a special coach reserved for him alone. It was quite an event for the community, and for the Senator too, when his private car first came to rest on his own rails in the yard of the great new United Verde smelter at Clarkdale.

The life and acts of William Andrews Clark can better be understood in the knowledge that he was a product of an era of financial buccaneering, an era which produced such noted or notorious operators as Jim Fisk, Boss Tweed, Daniel Drew, Jay Gould, John D. and William Rockefeller, H. H. Rogers, J. P. Morgan, James Stillman and Thomas Lawson. To gain great riches one had to be sharp, always hard and sometimes ruthless.

Clark was sharp, and as hard or ruthless as each situation encountered seemed to demand. In his business dealings he was careful to act within the letter of the law, though a burning ambition led him to walk a dangerous path in the political field. While in his twenties he had gained a solid foothold in Montana; at the age of thirty-three he had become known as the leading capitalist in the territory. He began to think in terms of power. When he first began to taste success he made the boastful promise that one day he would be the richest man in Montana and a United States senator. At these words his friends smiled pityingly, while his enemies sneered. But that promise he kept.

Before he was forty he was thrice a millionaire. Before he was fifty he was a multi-millionaire and the owner of the United Verde, which he prized so highly that a few years later, long before it had attained its peak, he flatly refused for it an offer of fifty million dollars made by the "Standard Oil Trust" — the Amalgamated Copper Company.

During the sixty years of his active pursuit of wealth he developed and acquired enterprises which made fortunes in commerce, banking, lumbering, manufacturing, public utilities, real estate, railroading, stock raising, sugar refining, and mining — especially in mining. He owned during his lifetime many mines; six of these each returned millions.

And chief among these mines, of course, was the great United Verde at Jerome, for nearly four decades the Senator's especial pride.

Clark's high confidence in himself is well illustrated by the fact that he never went afield to invest money that could be placed into an enterprise of his own. If he found that he had more cash than he needed for his current operations and reserves he would consider something new. The largest investment he ever held in any commercial enterprise, outside his own businesses, was in Union Pacific bonds; finally tiring of competition with rival railroad to the west coast, he sold the Salt Lake road to the competitor, taking in payment a million dollars in cash and twenty-nine million in bonds.

Through the operation of the line he also gained a son-in-law, Marius de Brabant, third husband of his daughter Mary. De Brabant had been his manager of traffic.

During the years of his fame as an immensely wealthy industrialist, there was much speculation as to the dollar value of the Senator's possessions. Though it doesn't matter much in an era when billions are spoken of almost as often as millions, the question still is asked. The appraised value of Clark's probated estate is meaningless, as prior to his death he had distributed to his sons, daughters and wife the greater portion of his wealth. Taking his various enterprises at a conservative earning value, it can be estimated that at the peak of his operations his holdings were worth not less than three hundred millions. Other estimators have claimed he was worth up to half a billion. Anyway, he was almost rich enough to satisfy his ambitions. He was classed by Senator Robert La Follette as among the hundred capitalists who ruled America, and Bernard Baruch once named him as one of America's richest twelve.

It has often been said that Senator Clark was among the least philanthropic of America's millionaires; that he lived for himself and his family alone, and that little was left to remind the world of his accomplishments. No endowments of note were established, and only a few memorials, the principal one being the William Andrews Clark art collection in the Corcoran Gallery of Art in Washington.

William Andrews Clark was born in Pennsylvania in 1839, of Scottish-Irish-Huguenot ancestry. His father was a farmer. He moved with his family to Iowa when he was seventeen. He preferred a school room to a farm, and entered an academy to prepare for teaching. He taught school in Missouri in 1859, and took up the study of law. It has been claimed without proof that Clark fought with the secessionists during the first year of the war between the states, but whether with regulars or irregulars the bearers of the tale did not claim to know. Clark would never confirm this story.

The only military duty Clark is known to have performed was in 1877, when the governor of Montana commissioned him a major under instructions to enlist men to join the federal cavalry then in pursuit of Nez Perce Indians who had massacred some white settlers in the Bitter Root Valley. Clark responded with enthusiasm and raised three companies of horse militia. Before he made union with General Miles' cavalry the regulars had already fought a violent battle, in which seventy-five of the troops were killed or wounded. With other troops coming up behind them the Indians fled, subsequently to be captured by General Miles. Clark's volunteers saw no fighting, but the incident remained a bright spot in his memory and was recited in the memoirs of his career prepared for the Montana Society of Pioneers.

In 1862 Clark moved west to Colorado, and performed manual labor in mines near Denver. He hoarded what money was left after the purchase of bare necessities. The fever for gold was contagious, and he began to plan for a mine of his own. News of a gold strike took him to Montana the following spring. He and a partner located a claim near Bannock, and were luckier than most, for they took out several thousand dollars in placer gold.

By fall of 1863 Clark had the capital he needed for the first step toward his fortune. Merchandise was selling in the gold camps at fantastic prices, and Clark perceived an easier way to gather gold than to grub for it. He persuaded his partner to join him in buying a team and wagon, and they traveled to Salt Lake City for a load of staple goods. The profit from this venture was substantial.

The next spring the partners returned to their claim, and worked it profitably during the summer months. With enough capital to enable him to abandon manual labor for good, Clark sold his interest in the claims.

Inspired by the success of his first small venture in trading, Clark bought and hired more wagons and freighted in more goods, buying as far east as Missouri and as far west as Portland, Oregon. His capital increased. Before he was thirty he was well established as a wholesale and retail merchandiser, he had contracted for mail routes, he was buying and selling livestock, he had become a money lender (two percent per month was the going rate), and he was keeping his eyes open for mining properties which held possibilities for future profit.

In 1869 Clark returned to Pennsylvania to marry Katherine Stauffer, the sweetheart of his younger days. He brought his bride to Montana and the couple settled at Deer Lodge where his businesses were centered. At the age of thirty-three Clark was president of a bank and owner or partner in various other enterprises. That year he visited Butte, then in a decline because of the exhaustion of the gold placers which had been the foundation of its initial prosperity. Clark was certain the camp's future lay in its mineral lodes, but that with no reduction machinery at hand the lodes could be considered only long range prospects. He bided his time, bought and manipulated, and after the coming of the railroad made large profits from mines and mills which had cost him but little. He took time out to study geology at Columbia University.

By 1895 the little man with the red hair had become one of the best known and wealthiest men in the West, and due for further riches, as his United Verde mine in Arizona was swinging into production.

Clark continued to perform energetically, no holds barred. He traveled extensively with his family, and became a polished internationalist. He fell in love with France. He maintained an affable front with his old cronies while gradually withdrawing from the rough-and-tumble life of the mining camps into his new world. He established his head office and home in New York.

It had been in 1885 that Clark, while representing his state at the New Orleans World Exposition, saw exhibits of Arizona ores. Outstanding among them for sheer beauty and high metal content was one labeled "United Verde Copper Company, Jerome." He had an investigation made of the United Verde, and the following year made a personal visit, where he met Frederick Murray. Clark liked what he saw and smelled a bargain in the offing. He made friends with Murray, and characteristically waited.

He was in Paris when in the fall of 1887 United Verde affairs reached their most critical stage, and when he arrived home found that serious negotiations for the sale of the mines were being conducted with Dr. James Douglas. When the terms offered by Douglas were turned down, Clark with Murray's aid was on hand to step into the breach.

In the fall of 1888 ores were again being smelted in the little two-furnace plant in the gulch above Jerome. This was mainly for experimental purposes, but the operation returned a profit too. Clark brought in one of the new fangled diamond drills, and drilling combined with new underground explorations disclosed rich ore bodies not before known.

When in 1892 a rail line was built from Ash Fork to Phoenix, Clark immediately put in a connecting twenty-seven mile narrow gauge road over the mountain to Jerome, and began to build the new smelter which became operational in 1895.

The United Verde became Clark's great pride. Before the turn of the century shares in the company which had been bought for a dollar were returning twelve dollars a year in dividends. Clark declared to his sons and daughters that the United Verde was to remain in the Clark family for all time. As king of his domain he expected to be obeyed.

Money had enabled Clark to achieve all his ambitions except the one he coveted most — the office of United States Senator. Money should be able to obtain that too. With his twenty-six year old son Charles as his campaign manager, in 1899 he began to pull the strings which would induce the Montana state legislature to elect him to the Senate. He had been a candidate as early as 1889 and again in 1893, but failed because of the opposition of his enemies.

Marcus Daly, head of the Anaconda Copper Mining Company, was Clark's chief political opponent, but he had the support of F. Augustus Heinze. Daly and Heinze were the chief opponents in the notorious conflict known as the war of the copper kings. Clark had avoided becoming involved in this war, standing by to play either side as circumstances might indicate. Later he was to turn against Heinze.

The battle in the Montana legislature over the election of a senator in 1899 produced the substance for a luridly propagandized period in the state's history. Clark was accused of spending a million dollars in bribes and hirings to bring about the vote which elected him. An attempt was made to have a grand jury indict him for bribery. This failed, but his attorney was indicted. Charles Clark escaped indictment at that time too, but later he was not to be so fortunate.

Clark went to Washington in 1900 to claim a seat in the Senate, but through the direction of Marcus Daly the charges of bribery, perjury and fraud were placed before the Senate committee on privileges and elections. Realization of the unfavorable result that the hearings would probably bring caused Clark to resign.

He returned home after this defeat to lay plans for another try. Marcus Daly was sick with an ailment which caused his death in the fall of 1900. The next year the Montana legislature again elected Clark to the Senate, and this time he was seated without opposition, serving until 1907. He did not enjoy duties attached to the job and thereafter sought no public office. He did aspire to appointment as ambassador to France, but under a Republican administration and in view of the scandal surrounding his first election to the Senate he soon realized the futility of such a desire.

During this period Clark prepared to make New York City his permanent home. He built a mansion on Fifth Avenue. Its design was a hybrid product of French and American architects, with strange looking and ornate towers. By the standards of conventional architecture its appearance was bizarre. It contained 121 rooms, including four art salons. It had thirty-one bath rooms. Its interior was sumptuously furnished with hardwood from various parts of the world, and many elaborate carvings, some gold-leafed. Its bronze stair rails were gold plated, and it was lavishly furnished with period pieces and rich imported carpetings, rugs and draperies. Building and furnishings cost the Senator fifteen million dollars, not including his paintings and other art objects.

His Fifth Avenue neighbors ridiculed the mansion, but William Andrews Clark made the Social Register.

His sons didn't like the house either, and as executors of their father's estate sold it as soon as title could be passed. It was dismantled to make way for an apartment house.

The Senator's collection of paintings and drawings included several Corots, and other famous European artists represented were Rembrandt, Millett, Rousseau, Chardin, Van Dyck, Titian, Hogarth, Daubigny, Hals, Perugino, Monticelli, Daumier, Degas, Gainsborough, Reynolds and Raeburn. American artists were represented by such masters as Abbey, Blakelock, Innes, Eakins and Wyant.

Clark's tastes ran to the conventional; he chose paintings that appealed to him, and but few of the productions called modern found their way into his galleries.

In addition to the paintings there was an imposing collection of Gobelin and Gothic tapestries, rugs, laces, faience, sculptures and other antiques.

The Senator was almost as proud of his art collection as he was of the United Verde. No one accused him of being a connoisseur, which bothered him not at all. He bought what pleased him, and let opinion — or cost — be hanged. He would spend hours in the gallery which housed his Corots, enjoying those particularly which portrayed lush scenes, such as "Ronde de Nymphes" and "Le Lac de Terni." Such landscapes as these and his "Apres la Pluie" by Rosseau reminded him of the ponds and forests of his boyhood days in Pennsylvania and Iowa, when he could walk barefoot in the cool spring grasses and wade in the waters. A nickel had seemed as large a sum of money then as a million dollars did now, but in his fading years he knew those days to have been the happiest of his life.

Clark willed his entire art collection to the Metropolitan Museum of Art in New York, with the stipulation that it must remain intact as the William Andrews Clark collection, and be housed separately. If refused on those terms, as it was, the collection should under the same provisions be offered to the Corcoran Gallery of Art in Washington. If still rejected the collection was to be sold at public auction.

After rejection by the Metropolitan Museum, Clark's widow and his three living daughters provided seven hundred thousand dollars to build two additional wings to the Corcoran gallery. There the Senator's art collection, valued by the gallery at five million dollars at the time it was placed, came to rest.

The Senator was twice married. Katherine Stauffer Clark died in 1893, after bearing three sons, Charles Walker Clark, William Andrews Clark, Jr., and one who died in infancy, and two daughters, Mary and Katherine. Clark's second romance was the occasion of wide publicity and his enemies strove mightily to make a scandal of it. Anna La Chapelle, a Butte girl, daughter of a boarding house keeper, was still a minor when taken under the Senator's wing following the death of his first wife, placed in the care of a chaperon, educated in Paris and given a continental polish. Clark visited her every year and eventually married her. By this union there were two daughters, Andree, who died while still a school girl, and Huguette.

One of the characteristics of the Senator which impressed men with less endurance or propensity for kingship was his refusal to delegate full authority to any one in the supervision of his many interests. Not until his declining years did he give more than nominal executive authority to any man, and then only through his sons. The status of the men in operational supervision of the United Verde at the time Clark's new smelter at Jerome commenced operation furnished an example.

From Butte Clark sent John L. Thompson to supervise the smelting and Joseph L. Giroux to operate the mine. Giroux was subsequently made superintendent of the entire operation. Liaison between these two and Clark was established through Henry J. Allen, also from Butte, who had the duties of office manager, financial and political agent, observer and reporter, but without firm appointive title or executive authority. All problems of any importance and many that were minor were referred to Clark, first by wire in codes which he had prepared for his exclusive use, followed by written reports in detail. Such a climate was ideal for disagreements and even battles between the minor officials. Allen was in a continuous state of frustration and bitterness, the finale of which was tragedy.

When, early in the century, Charles W. Clark was named general manager of the United Verde matters began to improve, but still friction continued. The Senator was well aware of this situation, but he believed in rivalry between his men. It would keep them on their toes.

Clark personally kept close watch over his enterprises. His New York office was loaded with reports, daily, weekly, monthly and annual, from each of his many operations. He made regular tours from New York to his Montana, Utah, California and Arizona properties to confirm the reports. This continued until the last year of his life.

Not in the history of America has there been a like example of a man of vast wealth keeping such close individual control of a galaxy of operations from youth to old age. After his first business ventures Clark established no partnerships or financial liaisons outside his own family. He allowed no shares in any of his many corporations to be distributed to the public. He issued no bonds or mortgages. He was absolute monarch.

Though it had been the Senator's deepest wish that the ownership of the United Verde be forever retained in the family, after his death in 1925 a feud developed between the two elder daughters and the two sons. In the battle for control the sons remained on top while they lived, but following Charles W. Clark's death in 1933 and William A. Clark Junior's death the following year, the situation changed. Both the American Smelting and Refining Company and Phelps Dodge Corporation began bidding for United Verde shares, and heirs holding a majority were found ready to sell. Phelps Dodge won out and took control of United Verde properties and assets, including ninety million pounds of copper bars stored at Clarkdale, at a cost of about twenty million dollars. At that time the world had only begun to recover from the great depression; copper was still a drug on the market, and advisors of the two sisters convinced them that copper would never again be scarce in supply or worth more than ten cents a pound.

Phelps Dodge, as the company officials well knew, had obtained a real bargain. They became owners of the United Verde just forty-seven years after Dr. James Douglas, acting for the old Phelps, Dodge and Company, had so narrowly missed accomplishing the same end. The purchasers doubled their money before the last ore was hoisted and the furnace fires at Clarkdale finally were dead.

With the sale of the United Verde the last of the important mining and industrial properties the Senator had acquired passed from the hands of his heirs, as the Montana properties had been sold to the Anaconda Company in 1928.

The theme of the story of William Andrews Clark can be sketched with brevity: The ambitious youth answering the call of the West with a burning desire to achieve wealth, position and fame by whatever means available; the goal achieved.

That theme could easily be expanded into a book. In fact, one disgruntled person who had been in the confidential employ of the Clarks in Montana did write a book about Clark and the members of his immediate family — a scandalous screed in which the author appeared to have found in most of the members of the clan a profusion of evil and a dearth of good. The writer awaited the death of the elder Clark and his two sons before publishing this sorry work.

I was employed in the administrative department of the United Verde Copper Company and its successor for four decades with frequent contact with the Senator and Charles W. Clark, was the latter's Arizona secretary, and had opportunity to closely observe their operations. The Clarks were generous to their towns and employees — too generous in the eyes of other mining men, who were astonished and a bit dismayed at the amounts spent not only for the needs but for the comforts and pleasures of their employees. To those who had to account to watchful stockholders for all expenditures this was an example they could not match. Clark was the first to introduce an eight hour day in the mines of Montana, and claimed to have been instrumental in having a territorial law passed instituting the eight hour day in the mines of Arizona.

Everything derogatory that could be said of William Andrews Clark has no doubt been said. Few have bothered to search for virtues since his obituaries were written. But those who have lived in his Arizona towns, or visited those towns; those who have seen the ruins of Jerome and the great mine and smelter which were monuments to this one man's endeavor, can find something good to say. They must give him credit for having been a man of keen foresight, progressive spirit, and solid accomplishment.

United Verde Smelter and Roasting Levels, 1898.

The Man from Long Island

JAMES ALLAN MACDONALD

"A gentleman of the old school" his obituary read. James Allan Macdonald deserved the distinction conveyed by that characterization.

This man who served the United Verde Copper Company in an official capacity longer than any other man only occasionally visited the property which had returned his investment hundreds of times over. In fact, I recall only two such visits, one being after the new Clarkdale smelter was in operation and he came to view its wonders. He was past seventy years old then. His last visit was after Senator Clark's death when he was eighty-one. He was tall, gray haired, dignified and courteous. Though still erect he was slow and careful of movement, supporting himself with a gold headed cane.

He was a credit to the Clan Macdonald. Descendent of highland warriors, his ancestors had reached North America from Scotland in pre-revolutionary days, and his family had become well established among the city's distinguished pioneers. Born in 1842, he was a graduate of Columbia College with bachelor of arts and master degrees. Then he went to war with a company of New York volunteers. After the war was over he studied at Yale, and added to his honors a bachelor of science degree. From the same university in later life he received an honorary degree of bachelor of philosophy.

Macdonald had a keen business sense, and became associated with a number of enterprises. He was president of the Queen Insurance Company for many years, and a director of the Royal Insurance Company. He was also a director of the Commercial Trust Company of New Jersey, and had interests in many other sound enterprises.

He was not averse to "taking a flyer" if his analysis indicated that the chance for success outweighed the possibility of failure. He was therefore receptive to purchasing stock in the United Verde when he read the glowing reports of William Murray, Frederick Tritle and F. F. Thomas and subscribed for 12,500 shares. In recognition of his reputation and firm financial position the directors elected him the company's first president.

When the company ran into trouble after its first attempt at operation, and William A. Clark met with the directors on that February day in 1888, all but Macdonald were eager to commit themselves to acceptance of his offer. He neither assented nor dissented; he would give the plan consideration. The deal was finally closed without Clark having obtained an option on Macdonald's stock. The man from Flushing felt that with Clark's energy and unlimited financial resources the mine was nearer to being an investment than a gamble.

Throughout the Montana millionaire's operation of the United Verde, Macdonald held a larger interest in the property than anyone outside the Clark family. In fact, William A. Clark and his progeny eventually acquired all other shares. Finally they acquired Macdonald's too when the Clark brothers bought these only outstanding shares from the Macdonald estate.

When William A. Clark took the office of president, he chose Macdonald as vice president, a position he held until his final days. Recognizing the astute management of the company under Clark, he supported the owner in most of his decisions, though he never hesitated to give advice. His aristocratic birth and mien balanced the up-from-the-soil and the self-made do-it-yourself character and personality of Clark and the earthiness of the company's operating staff, notable especially in the development period when taught-by-experience men were in the majority.

Macdonald's canniness paid off richly. Ten years after the Senator took control his 12,500 shares were returning dividends at the rate of $150,000 a year. By the time those shares passed from his estate they had returned upward of three million dollars.

For many years a widower, Macdonald's companion, business associate and secretary was his daughter Flora. Why she was so christened will be apparent to the readers of the history of Scotland. Flora Macdonald was a Scottish heroine, who gained fame through an act of heroism and devotion in the year 1746. When Prince Charles Edward Stuart, pretender to the throne of England, was defeated by the Duke of Cumberland in the bloody battle of Culloden Moor, Flora dressed the prince in women's clothing, passed him off as her maid, and helped him escape to the Isle of Skye. From there, after many hardships, he succeeded in reaching France.

Flora could not keep secret her part in the prince's escape; she was arrested and imprisoned in the Tower of London. But the hates of war were cooling and she was soon released. The battle of Culloden was the climax of the efforts of the Stuarts to regain the throne of England. Nevertheless, patriotic fervor long burned in the breasts of the Scots, and among those they placed on the pinnacle of devotion and heroism was Flora Macdonald.

She married one of her own name, Allan Macdonald, and in 1773 they emigrated to the new world.

James Allan Macdonald died at his home in Flushing, Long Island, in 1929 at the age of 86. His daughter, Flora Macdonald Bonney, survived him and inherited his estate.

Pipeline from Walnut Springs that supplied the town of Jerome with fresh water. (Jerome Historical Society, E. Hopkins Col.)

HENRY J. ALLEN

The Man from Louisiana

HENRY JAMES ALLEN

In the decade beginning with the construction of the new United Verde smelter in 1895, no name in central Arizona with the exception of Clark was more prominent than that of H. J. Allen.

He was always colorful, frequently unpredictable, and was remembered long after other characters of early Jerome were forgotten.

He was William A. Clark's man, and had been sent to Jerome from Butte. Beyond those facts no one in the mining town knew anything at all about Allen's past. Least of all did they know that his name was not Allen — that Henry James Alston had changed his name in order that he might not continue to cause embarrassment to the aristocratic Alstons of Louisiana, who had agreed never to mention his name again.

In addition to their plantation interests the Alstons owned a river boat which engaged in freight and passenger traffic on the Mississippi from New Orleans to Illinois. In his early twenties young Henry acted as purser on this boat, enjoying the travel and the excitement of the hell-for-leather river feuds and competition.

Alston was an extrovert who found pleasure in contest, and fell naturally into political affairs. In an election campaign he and an opponent fought a duel in which the opponent was killed. Though Alston was not indicted for murder a demand was made, in which his family assented, that he leave Louisiana and not come back. He embarked on a north bound boat to search for a position in which his political and public relations talents could be employed.

He had married Annabelle Wright — called Belle — a girl who was a descendant of the Polks of North Carolina, the family which had produced a president of the United States. They had an infant daughter Ella Gayle. Belle Alston remained failthful to her dashing husband, and awaited only the establishment of a new home to join him.

To complete the severance of family ties, Alston took the name of Allen, and he retained that name the rest of his life.

71

The Union Pacific railroad was building West, and Allen was employed as advance agent for the road. His business was to travel ahead of rail, adjusting right of way questions, making friends for the line, locating the best spots for stations, employing agents, and advertising the fact that Union Pacific would sell tickets to any place in the world which could be reached by water or rail traffic.

In 1885 Butte, Montana, was becoming a young city, as was the neighboring smelter community of Anaconda. On arriving there Allen visited the mine owners, to sing the praises of his approaching road and solicit business for the new rail line. Marcus Daly of the Anaconda company was impressed with Allen's evident ability and talent for persuasion, and offered him a job. Tired of being on the move and longing for a permanent home Allen accepted. He sent for his wife and daughter and established a home in Anaconda.

His nominal title was chief timekeeper, a job which kept him in touch with the employees, but his duties were largely political. He was a good organizer, and he had a great opportunity in Butte and Anaconda to develop his ability.

When in 1888 William A. Clark was successful in securing the Democratic nomination for delegate to congress, Clark found himself opposed by T. H. Carter, a Republican who had the support of Daly. Clark had made an enemy of Daly when, in Daly's early days in Butte he had tried to persuade his backers to dismiss him. Clark also found that a young man by the name of Allen was in charge of organizing the campaign against him, securing orators, arranging torchlight parades, directing newspaper advertising, and performing other political chores. To Clark's amazement and distress he was beaten, even in Butte where he had been expecting his strongest support.

Because of Daly's opposition, which had been carried to the limits of legality, he had become even more Clark's enemy, and toward his enemies Clark barred no holds that could be justified by the questionable mores of his time and location. His next move in this political war would be to remove Allen as an opponent — this man whose clever manipulations had been largely responsible for his defeat. He arranged a secret conference with Allen, offered him more money than Daly was paying him, and promised him a responsible job at the new mine he had just acquired down in Arizona as soon as it had been developed to the point where Allen's talent could be used.

THE MAN FROM LOUISIANA

Being fully aware of Clark's unlimited wealth and his shrewdness, and with an eye ever cocked for the main chance, Allen entered Clark's employ in a capacity similar to the one in which he had served Daly.

Clark kept his promise. In 1891 he assigned Allen to the United Verde. Allen sent his wife and daughters, now two, to Louisiana to remain there until a home could be built in Jerome. A year later they joined him, together with two colored servants from the home plantation, a man and wife. The trip to Jerome over the wagon road from Ash Fork contributed to the dislike Belle Allen had for the West, so far from the comforts of her girlhood. But she was a good wife and endured the hardships with little complaint.

At that time Clark was operating at full blast the two little furnaces at the United Verde, turning out a million pounds of copper a month. Frank Murphy of Prescott and his associates were building a railroad from Ash Fork to Prescott and Phoenix. In 1893 the Santa Fe, Prescott and Phoenix line reached Prescott. Allen assisted in the acquisition of a right of way from Chino Valley to Jerome for a railroad. Contracts for construction of the United Verde & Pacific Railroad Company's narrow gauge line were let in 1894, and the road was completed in 1895. Materials for a fine new smelter at last could be transported to Jerome by rail.

Allen's position with the United Verde was nominally office manager and financial agent, but his most important function was, as it had been in Butte, political.

Handsome, of medium height, moustached and with a fine head of dark hair, Allen was possessed of a charming manner when charm was desirable. Though known in Jerome among mine and smelter employees as tough and hardboiled, he made friends easily with the politicians, bankers and business men of Prescott and the capitol city of Phoenix. He was popular with the ladies; he was a good drinker and with his friends was known as a convivial companion. He was empowered by Clark to keep a well filled sack for use in gaining political and legal ends. In the days when the territory was largely undeveloped money talked with a loud voice.

The story is told that Allen was responsible for one of those derogatory names sometimes acquired by legislatures — such as Arizona's "thieving thirteenth" of 1885. He was particularly interested in keeping down mine taxation, obtaining other legislation favorable to mines — especially the United Verde — and defeating laws that would be unfavorable. In some manner a bundle of bank notes which he had drawn for use at a legislative session in Phoenix had been marked by unfriendly hands, a maneuver intended to prove that Allen was spending money in an improper way.

When the marked money began to show up the cry was raised that the United Verde had been caught in an act of bribery. Allen had a ready answer. During this particular trip he had been making purchases for the mine, including some harness stock, and when accused he blandly replied that his money had been spent for the purchase of mules. When it was claimed that some of the legislators had been spending the marked money, the lawmakers were laughingly called "mules" and that session became known as "the mule legislature".

In the late nineties Allen's health began to fail; he was subject to periods of depression, and his relations with Clark began to deteriorate. More and more he resented the criticisms the United Verde owner was wont frequently to make of actions which Allen had taken. He felt that his services to Clark had been indispensable, and should have been rewarded, if not with substantial compensation at least with favorable acknowledgment. Following the disastrous fire of 1898, when a hundred business and residence buildings in the heart of the town were consumed Allen received harsh criticism because, the Senator claimed, he had not been fully informed by wire of the damage caused by the blaze the day it occurred. It developed that Allen had sent a telegram containing the facts in which he had used a number of coded phrases, but in the rush of messages the code words, synthetic scrambles of consonants and vowels, had been omitted either by the local or a relay telegraph office. Though the Senator blasted the sending of an incomplete message as a piece of stupidity, he failed to apologize when he was shown that Allen was not at fault. His reply to his agent's bitter protest was that he naturally did not know that the message was incomplete, and he was justified in saying what he did for the reason that if Allen had sent such a message it would have been stupid. This infuriated Allen, who considered Clark's response arrant dissimulation, and he replied that any further such ungrateful and baseless accusations would result in his resignation.

The fact that Allen had lost his house and everything in it, and that his family had been made temporarily homeless, contributed to his disturbed state of mind. After the construction of the new smelter was commenced in 1895, his responsibilities had become more complicated, and more and more he had been tied down to the office routine he disliked. The work he had been doing in the political field was curtailed, some of it having been entrusted to attorneys, and this too Allen resented.

One circumstance which culminated toward the end of the decade, particularly agravating and damaging to Allen, was the so-called Allaire affair. Allen had employed Herbert Allaire in 1897 as a stenographer-clerk for his office. Allaire held this position through 1899. He then showed up in New York as a witness against Clark in a suit which George A. Treadwell had brought to force an accounting for alleged misuse of company funds, and to prevent reincorporation of the United Verde Copper Company in another state, a move made by Clark to avoid heavy New York corporation taxes. Allaire claimed that Clark had made an intimate of him during the Senator's visits to Jerome, and that in long talks with Clark he learned many things regarding activities that were supposedly secret. Clark branded Allaire a damned traitorous liar, and had the clerk's past life traced, discovering that he was an ex-convict whose real name was Steele. Clark censured Allen for having employed and harbored a criminal and a spy.

After the turn of the century Allen's health continued to deteriorate, and his eyesight began to fail. Having finally made the Senate, Clark had less time to spend in the details of operation and gave Charles W. Clark more responsibility and the title of general manager. Allen didn't get along well with Charles, who was out to make a record of good management on his own. He began to brood, and came to the conclusion that his usefulness to his family, whom he had always indulged and adored, was coming to an end. His family had been increased by the addition of a son and by the marriage of his daughter Gayle to Tom Campbell, handsome young postmaster and mine operator of Jerome.

In December 1903 his resentment against Senator Clark culminated in a decision to write an exposé of the political manipulations of which he had been a part under the direction of Clark, both in Montana and Arizona. The exposé was written and held for release at an opportune time.

The time came soon. When Allen received word early in January, 1904, that Charles W. Clark was to arrive on January 8 with the Senator's New York auditor and Will L. Clark of Butte (no relation) he concluded that his time was up. On January 6 he mailed to a Phoenix muck-raking sheet the exposé he had prepared.

Not until then did he begin to ponder what the results of this action might be. He had failed, he now realized, to consider the effect on his family. They would suffer disgrace, and the vengeance of the Clarks would be wreaked on Allen himself.

He must have the exposé back. Through the United Verde's Prescott attorney he tried desperately to have the mailing reclaimed. This effort was fruitless.

Charles W. Clark and his party arrived in Jerome as planned. Allen was not at the station to meet them. After they had breakfasted they went to the company office. Allen was not there either. But on his desk was found an envelope addressed to Charles. Inside was a single sheet of paper on which was inscribed this message:

"When you receive this I will be no more. H. J. A."

Alarmed, Charles had inquiry made of Allen's wife regarding his whereabouts. Her husband, she said, had gone to his ranch at Peck's Lake in the valley. He had been acting strangely, which had alarmed her. She had immediately communicated her concern to Tom Campbell, who had quickly saddled a horse and started for the lake.

Charles endeavored to get a telephone call through to the Allen ranch, but was informed that the line was dead. He then learned from the livery stable where Allen boarded his driving team that their owner had left an hour before. Charles ordered a team harnessed for him, then called Dr. Woods, the company physician, and ordered him to meet him at the stable. Together they drove as fast as possible to the Allen ranch, where they arrived an hour later.

Tom Campbell was there, standing on the front porch.

"Mr. Allen is inside," he said. "He has barred the door and rolled a bed behind it. He says he's going to kill himself, and I think he means it. I doubt if my pleas have done any good."

As Charles and Dr. Woods hurriedly advanced, Allen appeared at a window. A gun was in his hand. Charles called to him that he wanted to talk.

Allen's response was to place the muzzle of the gun to his chest and pull the trigger.

Returning to his office Charles wired his father a three word message, a record for brevity.

"Allen died today."

He immediately started an investigation, and learned through the

company's Prescott attorneys of Allen's desperate effort to recover something which had been mailed to a Phoenix scandal sheet. Charles had no
difficulty in surmising what the mailing must contain.

He sent a long coded message to the Senator, and received an order to
recover the mailing, at whatever cost. Charles put the attorneys to work,
and received word three days later that their efforts had been successful.

To Charles, who had spent large sums for his father in political cam-
paigns, the cost of the recovery must have seemed modest. It was only
ten thousand dollars.

Gayle Allen Campbell, daughter of Henry James Allen,
and wife of Thomas E. Campbell.

GEORGE W. HULL

The Man from Massachusetts
GEORGE WILLIAM HULL

"Make-a-Million" Hull they called him, because he had sworn not to let up on his wheelings and dealings until he could claim wealth of a million dollars.

The name "Hull" will live as long as Jerome lives in such designations as Hull Canyon, Hull Springs, Hull Avenue, and Hull Copper Company. There had been a Hull store and a Hull ranch and a Hull freight line. The man who bore the name still lives in the memory of the oldest old timers of Jerome and the Verde Valley.

This is the way a newspaper reporter at the turn of the century described George W. Hull:

"He is sixty-three years old, slender, wiry and gray. He has a great faculty for acquiring property. At one time he owned nearly all the property in the Verde District. He organized the original United Verde Extension, which he believes is a veritable bonanza. He has taken an active interest in politics and is a consistent Democrat and silverman. He has been a member of the territorial legislature. In his early days he practiced law, and served a term as justice of the peace. He was throught to be a confirmed bachelor until he took a wife two years ago; now he has an heir to the prospective Hull millions. He is one of the characters of Yavapai County."

Hull was seventy-three years old when I met him first in 1912, but he was still vigorous and active and looking forward to the time which for years had been his goal — when he could retire a millionaire. That time was not so very far away; he made his million, but he did not live long to enjoy it.

George William Hull was born at Berry, Massachusetts on November 4, 1839. He came West at the age of 19, first to Nevada, where he built and operated a toll road into the then booming town of Hamilton. From Nevada he drifted down to Arizona, spending some time at Flagstaff, where he operated a store and got into the freighting business.

After the railroad came he took his teams and wagons down to the Verde Valley, intrigued by the rumors regarding the richness of the Black Mountains and the ranchers' paradise along the Verde River. He did some freighting between Camp Verde and Jerome, bought a ranch in the Middle Verde area and established a store and freighting business at Aultman at the junction of the Camp Verde and Cherry Creek roads, midway on the freighting run.

Hull was extremely acquisitive, a shrewd trader and adept at finding bargains. In 1883, the year the first little United Verde smelter was started, he began to acquire property in Jerome. He established a store there and took up permanent residence. He married Margaret Jane Barney in San Francisco in 1897, and to this union a son, George Benjamin Hull, was born in 1898. They were subsequently divorced. At the age of 64 he married again. Mary Hull became a partner in his various enterprises.

Hull continued with energy to buy, sell, and manipulate, and eventually came into ownership of much of the ground on which Jerome was built. His claims almost surrounded the United Verde. By the sale of lots in the town, being careful to retain all mineral rights twenty-five feet below the surface, he added to his capital sufficiently to start mining ventures. In 1899 he organized the United Verde Extension Gold, Silver & Copper Mining Company, later to become the bonanza United Verde Extension Mining Company — the fabulous UVX. Next he organized the Cleopatra Copper Company, then the Hull Copper Company. Cleopatra Hill acquired its name from one of the Hull claims. Out on the periphery of the centrally located group of claims Hull acquired the Columbia and King groups and organized the Consolidated King & Columbia Copper Mining Company.

Then sales promotions were commenced. Though Hull retained a majority of the shares in each company in return for his ownership, millions of shares were sold in England, Scotland and France as well as in the United States. The fame of Clark's United Verde had by then become world-wide, and the fact that the Hull and Cleopatra claims were contiguous to the United Verde stimulated sales.

In Walnut Canyon on the southeastern slope of Cleopatra Hill, later to be known as Hull Canyon, a tunnel was driven. When some ore was found, Hull built a little smelter in the canyon with Cleopatra Copper Company funds, which failed to return a profit. But the fact that is was there helped to sell Cleopatra shares.

THE MAN FROM MASSACHUSETTS

The most valuable of the Hull claims were those absorbed into the Hull Copper Company, incorporated in 1900. A lurid advertising campaign resulted in the sale of 2,400,000 shares, which returned to the company $72,000. Development work was commenced, and by July 1908 the money was exhausted. Hull continued to provide funds to work the property, signing notes as president to himself as an individual for the funds advanced.

Thus the situation remained until 1915. In that year the United Verde Extension opened up its bonanza. Rawhide Jimmy Douglas turned his eye to the favorably located Hull properties, and secretly began to buy Hull shares. The United Verde by that time had developed its ore bodies close to the boundary of the Hull claims and by the aid of some discreet diamond drilling discovered they contained valuable ores. The United Verde began negotiations with Hull to buy all his shares in his various companies. So did Douglas.

Some of the shares which had been sold had been re-acquired by the promoter and at that time more than three-quarters of Hull Copper Company shares were in Hull's name.

Hull resented the fact that he had relinquished his interest in the United Verde Extension in order to obtain funds to promote his other companies, and thought of the millions he had lost rankled. He leaked word to the United Verde officials that others were dickering for his stock holdings, also that a million dollars cash was the price. The United Verde made haste to bind Hull with an option at that figure.

The United Verde Extension then, through agents, organized the Hull Copper Company Stockholders Protective Association, the announced purpose being to protect the interest of the minority shareholders, alleging misappropriation of company funds by Hull, illegal issue of stock to himself, and general mismanagement. In the lawsuit which followed, Hull was savagely attacked by the opposition attorneys. On October 26, 1916, following an exhausting session on the witness stand defending his character and his management, George William Hull died suddenly, only a few days short of his seventy-seventh birthday.

Under court order 2,500,000 shares of Hull Copper Company shares standing in Hull's name were ordered returned to the treasury, enhancing the value of the remaining shares, of which United Verde Extension interests held more than a million.

In 1922 the Hull Copper Company, then officered by United Verde officials, in a deal with the United Verde Extension sold the Hull Copper claims to Louis S. Cates, an official of the Utah Copper Company, who acted as trustee during the liquidation of the company and distribution of its assets. The claims were divided between the two companies, those contiguous to the United Verde ore bodies subsequently being included in the extensive open pit operations. After all debts were paid the remaining cash assets were distributed among the stockholders at the rate of 27.7 cents per share.

The properties of the Cleopatra and Consolidated King & Columbia were subsequently taken over by the United Verde for debts.

Hull's widow and son followed a dream which Hull and his wife had nurtured for years and moved to California, which to mountain dwellers in those days was Paradise. At the widow's death the son inherited the Hull fortune.

As the newspaper reporter had stated, Hull was a "character". His peculiarities led to his being nicknamed "Granny". He was close fisted if not miserly, with an eye always open for an opportunity. He was intensely active; he hurried, he bounced. Every rock on every hill around Jerome became known to him. He paced and he measured. When he found something he believed had been overlooked by others he hired engineers, among them Tom Campbell, to confirm or disprove his hopes. In such manner he was able to locate some valuable fractions.

Hull didn't bother with lawyers. He was not a lawyer, but he did "practice law" to the extent that he drafted his own legal papers, and helped others with less experience with their deeds and mortgages and other minor legal matters. He once told me that he knew the law so far as it pertained to his business as well as any lawyer, and had been complimented by attorneys and judges for the manner in which he drafted legal documents. As a matter of fact, most of his legal instruments were well enough drawn to be acceptable even though the wording didn't always follow the usual legal forms.

He liked politics and enjoyed the work and prestige connected with public office. He served five terms in the lower house of the territorial legislature, one term as justice of the peace at Jerome, and for many years as a member of the Jerome town council including two years as mayor.

Charley Willard said that when he knew Hull in his early days in the valley he was a convivial type, and a singer. He was credited with introducing songs transported from older mining communities which were to ring in Jerome beer halls and at drinking parties for decades. Here is one, said to have originated in the Pennsylvania coal mines:

> *My sweetheart's a mule in the mine,*
> *I drive her with only one line;*
> *On the ore car I sit, and tobacco I spit*
> *All over my sweetheart's behind.*

Jerome was never quite the same after the ubiquitous George Hull was gone.

George W. Hull's Jerome; his store is shown right of center.

THOMAS E. CAMPBELL

14

Son of Arizona

THOMAS E. CAMPBELL

Prescott was seething with patriotic fervor that May morning in 1899. Buckey O'Neill with his company of Rough Riders was leaving for San Antone to train for the campaign in Cuba.

The company had assembled for a farewell ceremony in the court house plaza. There were cheers and tears. Speeches were made; tribute was paid to Buckey O'Neill, already famous throughout the Southwest as a fighting sheriff. He was not to return, but in later years was to be honored by a fine Borglum equestrian statue erected in that same place, depicting him in the charge up San Juan Hill where he met his death.

Prominent among the volunteers because of his six feet three height was young Tom Campbell, erect and handsome, surging with pride that he had this opportunity to serve his country as one of those who remembered the Maine.

The ceremony over, the company marched to the railroad station where it was to entrain. There Captain O'Neill was met by a determined woman.

"Tom cannot go with you," she decreed.

"Why, Mrs. Campbell?"

"Because he's not twenty-one yet, and as his parent and guardian I forbid you to take him. I don't want him in the army — I've seen too much of that life."

Reluctantly the captain informed Tom that he could not go along. Keenly disappointed, resentful that he could not join that hardy group of men in such an important undertaking, he returned to his job at the Prescott post office.

Thus a man who was to become one of Jerome's active citizens and one of Arizona's most distinguished public servants was denied the fulfilment of a cherished dream. He became restless, and was ready to leave for Jerome when offered a position in the post office of that flourishing mining camp.

Thomas E. Campbell was born in Prescott in 1878. His father, Daniel Campbell, was a veteran of the Civil and Indian wars and a long time army man, and had been chief warrant officer at Fort Whipple. His mother, born Eliza Flynn of Ireland's County Sligo, had been employed in the home of the paymaster general of the army's western division when Dan Campbell met and married her. Rather than leave Prescott he left the army when notified that he was to be transferred to San Francisco.

He and his wife conducted a dairy business and opened a small store in Prescott, where their three sons and a daughter grew to maturity.

Tom led the usual life of a boy in a frontier town. He was a member of the first graduating class of Prescott high school, where Fiorello La Guardia was to follow him. Then for three years he attended St. Mary's college in California, where he received training in geology.

Upon his return home he became an assistant in the Prescott post office, where he worked for a year before moving to Jerome in 1899. Jerome was a surging community with the largest population and the best payroll of any town north of Phoenix. Tom sensed opportunity there, and primed himself to seize it.

He immediately became active in the business, civic and social life of Jerome. With a partner he established a cigar store and news stand. Both the post office and the store were good listening posts, and much information was gained regarding the various mining properties in the area. Combining his knowledge of geology with a venturesome spirit he was soon actively engaged in promotions and developments.

In association with George W. Hull he arranged a deal on a property which Hull controlled. This transaction netted him ten thousand dollars, a nest egg which became a tremendously important factor in Tom's future.

One of the rival hose teams of Jerome's volunteer fire department was manned by prominent young men of the town, including its captain Tom Campbell. An outgrowth of the associations formed by this group was the Ananias Club, an exclusive, secret group which met almost nightly in the suite of Walter Miller, a relative of Senator Clark. Miller was manager of the T. F. Miller Company, operators of the big mercantile establishment known as "the Company Store". The incentive for the meeting was a poker game. Temperamentally Tom was well equipped to master the strategies of the game, and he added a neat sum to his nest egg.

Meanwhile another event occurred which was to have a great influence in molding Tom Campbell's future. In the summer of 1899 Ella Gayle Allen, daughter of Henry J. Allen, graduated from Mills College in Oakland, California, and returned home. Gayle Allen was a vivacious young lady with an engaging smile and charming manner; she was to become the belle of Jerome and a popular member of the social set of Prescott, where her family frequently spent holidays.

Gayle frequently called at the post office for the family mail, and she had made not more than half a dozen trips when Tom Campbell succumbed. He became a persistent suitor, but found the competition rough. Young ladies were scarce not only in Jerome but in Prescott as well, where the Allens mingled with families bearing such well known names as Ashurst, Goldwater, Hazeltine, Wells, Herndon, Norris, Windsor, Tritle and Heap. Among these families were a number of young men with whom Tom had to compete.

The Allen home was a focal point for the young men of Jerome, and Tom was a welcome guest at many social gatherings at the "top house" on "company row". But so were most of the other personable young men whom the expanding United Verde enterprise had attracted. Gayle's mother liked and approved of Tom, and of more importance, so did Gayle. Belle Allen gave the courtship a boost whenever she could, an accomplishment in itself, for Belle's principles were Victorian.

Henry J. Allen was more reluctant to give approval. Tom knew this when Gayle consented to marry him. But he hoped he had the means to impress the father, for steady gleanings from the Ananias Club had so added to his profit from the Hull deal that his bank book now showed a balance of more than twelve thousand dollars. Tom knew that while Henry J. believed romance to be a fine thing, he believed more strongly that a well stocked larder and wardrobe were essential to the perpetuation of romance's bloom. Any young man who wanted Allen's daughter would have to prove himself in the financial field.

The bank book spoke eloquent words. That a young man who had barely come of age could have accumulated twelve thousand dollars in a little more than a year really impressed Henry J. With his consent the wedding was set for June, 1900.

Then Belle Allen's Victorian training and a horse almost wrecked the wedding plans.

After the one carat stone was on Gayle's finger Belle permitted her daughter and Tom to take Sunday drives together, but she issued an edict that they must always be home before dark. On a Sunday two weeks before the wedding date Tom drove Gayle down to Peck's lake behind his fine team of bays, a slow trip down a winding mountain road and across the Verde River. They started back in ample time to reach Jerome before sunset, but one of the horses became lame and darkness had fallen before they arrived home.

Everything unraveled. No excuses or explanations were accepted. Belle ordered Gayle to pack her bags, and arranged for her to visit relatives in Louisiana and stay there until she learned how a gentlewoman should behave.

"Don't ever darken my door again," Belle ordered Tom in the true puritanical tradition.

Henry J., once the only barrier to the wedding, now became Tom's champion. After three days he finally calmed his wife down, and she consented to continue preparations for the wedding. Though Belle didn't know it, through her change of heart she set her daughter's feet on a path which was to enable her to become the gracious and respected first lady of a young and vigorous state.

The wedding was the top social occasion of Yavapai County that year. Gifts were gorgeous. Guests came from all over.

Father Allen arranged for as much comfort and privacy as possible on the trip out of Jerome. He had a special coach and baggage car coupled to the first train out. Tom and Gayle were the only passengers, they thought — until they learned that in the baggage section rode the encoffined corpse of a miner on his way to Prescott for burial.

That nearly ruined the trip for the bride. Under the influence of clinging Southern superstitions she was so badly shaken that she didn't regain her calm until the couple arrived in San Francisco two days later.

On their return trip they settled down happily to married life. In 1901 President McKinley appointed Thomas E. Campbell postmaster of Jerome. His salary of sixteen hundred a year was not enough to satisfy him. He worked harder than ever. He liked politics, and successfully entered the race for election to the house of representatives of the territorial legislature. He was the first native son to hold such an office. The victory started Tom Campbell on a political career which was to bring him the highest office a new state could give and to important posts in Washington and abroad.

Tom Campbell was a political idealist. His philosophy was in complete opposition to the operations of his father-in-law as representative of the demanding Senator Clark. Allen was a practicing politician of ability, with the money available to accomplish his ends. Campbell worked actively to combat Allen's activities, but even though they became political enemies their personal relations were friendly.

Campbell's most notable contribution to this session of the legislature was the introduction of an eight-hour law for workmen in hazardous industries. Senator Clark later claimed that he had sponsored this act out of consideration for the welfare of his employees and was responsible for its passage.

When the session was over Campbell returned to Jerome to continue his activities as postmaster, merchant, and mine operator. He also became government agent for the Yavapai-Apache Indians who had been allowed to return and live in the valley.

His two sons, Thomas Allen and Alexander Brodie, were born in Jerome in 1901 and 1904.

After Henry J. Allen's tragic death, both Belle and Gayle wanted to get away from Jerome. Belle and her children moved to California, and Campbell took Gayle to Prescott and established residence there. He continued his mining work; he managed the development work at the Haynes Copper Company at Jerome, financed by Boston capital, and also directed development work at three other mines.

But the lure of politics was strong. In 1907 he obtained appointment as assessor of Yavapai County, and again in 1909. Also he became a partner in an engineering firm, which suffered a heavy loss on a railroad contract. Tom was years in paying his share of the debt, which meant a long period of hardship for him and his family. He loathed the thought of bankruptcy, and refused to take that easy way out.

In 1912, in the special election following Arizona's admission to statehood, Tom Campbell was elected county assessor. He founded and was first president of the Arizona Assessor's Association. In the general election in November he was Republican candidate for representative to Congress, but was defeated. In 1914 he successfully ran for membership on the state tax commission, and was the only member of his party to win a state post.

During his two years on the tax commission Campbell gained popularity throughout the state, and in 1916 became a candidate for governor. When the votes were counted he was a few votes in the lead George W. P. Hunt, incumbent governor and Campbell's opponent contested. The superior court ruled Campbell the winner, but the supreme court reversed the decision. After serving a year without compensation Tom Campbell was returned to private life.

In 1918 Tom Campbell was again in the running, and was elected He was successful again in 1920. He was defeated in 1922.

For many years Campbell had been Republican national committee man, and his attendance and work at the national conventions had brought him wide recognition as a competent political figure and an eloquent and convincing speaker. Western governors and other prominent politicians began to promote him as the West's candidate for the vice presidency. He went to the 1920 convention with three hundred and sixty pledged votes. But after the stormy session which culminated in the nomination of Warren G. Harding, Campbell felt the need of avoiding further controversy. He waived the right to test his strength and relinquished his votes to Calvin Coolidge.

After his defeat in 1922 Campbell was requested by President Obregón of Mexico to visit him in the Mexican capital. During the visit Obregón asked him to try to bring about negotiations with the Department of State for recognition of his country by the United States, with whom Mexico was at the time "non grata". This Campbell did, with recognition of Mexico resulting the following year.

Campbell was appointed by the United States Senate as a member of a fact-finding committee charged with making a complete survey of Federal reclamation projects. This he undertook with Elwood Mead Based on their findings the Bureau of Reclamation was established Campbell was offered the post of director of the bureau, but declined and Mead was given the appointment. The great artificial lake above Hoover Dam was named for him.

President Coolidge offered Campbell the post of ambassador to Mexico, but being too poor to serve in a postion held traditionally by wealthy men he declined.

In 1926 President Coolidge appointed Campbell commissioner general to represent the United States at the Iberian-American exposition being developed at Seville in Spain. Campbell's popularity in Spain led to the conferring upon him of an honor that only one other American, Washington Irving, had been granted. He was made an honorary citizen of Seville

Campbell had a close association with Herbert Hoover, and after Hoover became President in 1928 he was offered a cabinet post. But financially unable to support such a prominent position in Washington he declined. Hoover then offered him the post of president of the Civil Service Commission, and this Campbell accepted. He held office through several months of the first Franklin D. Roosevelt administration by recommendation of Jim Farley, who commended Campbell for fine work in reorganization of the commission. Campbell resigned when Farley did, both of them disagreeing with Roosevelt's fiscal policies.

In 1930 Campbell again ran for governor of Arizona, at the urging of Herbert Hoover and Frank Lowden. But in those years Republican money was very, very scarce and campaign contributions were small. The campaign was lost.

During his political years Tom Campbell had many excellent offers of positions in other states, but he would not leave Arizona.

During the remainder of his life he worked with his old engineering firm on various projects. He was receiver for a large bankrupt farm project. He was technical director of the film "The Winning of Barbara Worth."

Thomas E. Campbell died in 1944, leaving thousands of friends, a widow and two sons to remember one who, though never rich, lived richly in the love, respect and confidence of his family and fellows.

Looking south on Main Street, c. 1920. Drug store on corner is present Mine Museum. It was the Fashion Saloon prior to passage of Arizona's prohibition law.

CHARLES W. CLARK

The Man from California

CHARLES WALKER CLARK

I first saw Charlie Clark in 1908.

I was curious to see this son of a multi-millionaire. I had heard of him first when he made a national sensation by whirling across the continent in a special train to reach the bedside of a dying wife.

The 1908 fair at Phoenix was billed as the greatest territorial fair Arizona had ever staged. No doubt it was. J. C. Adams of hotel fame and a political power was president of the fair commission, which also included Hugh Campbell, wealthy Coconino County sheep raiser. Shirley Christy, son of the founder of the Valley Bank and widely known rancher and sportsman, was the secretary. Many attractions were billed; Roy Knabenshue was to be there with his powered dirigible flying machine; the great pacing champion Dan Patch was coming to give exhibitions of his beauty, grace and speed; a big captive balloon would give the daring a ride a thousand feet into the air and a gorgeous view of the Salt River Valley through sparkling and smogless air. There would be a midway and hundreds of exhibits and horse races with well known pacers, trotters, runners, drivers and jockeys participating.

Temporary offices of the commission were in the basement of the original Adams hotel, which was to be consumed by fire two years later. As the assistant secretary of the fair commission, I was told to be on call for anything J. C. wanted. He would call me to his suite at eleven o'clock almost every morning to write a letter or two for the commission and several on personal matters. He would have had his breakfast in bed, and clad only in a night shirt would pace back and forth in his bare feet, shanks showing, while he dictated.

"Take a letter to Charles W. Clark at Jerome," he commanded one morning.

"Dear Charlie: Knowing your great interest in horses, having a stable of your own, the fair commission extends to you a cordial invitation to be present at the opening of the territorial fair in November. Dan Patch will be here, and you will have an opportunity to bet on some of the finest blooded racers and harness stock in the West. I'll have a box reserved for you, and I want you to be my special guest at the Adams."

Charlie Clark came to the fair. On the opening night there was a big reception in the spacious lobby of the hotel, with band music and general hilarity.

While I lingered in the background I saw J. C. and Shirley Christy emerge from the bar with a slender, fairly tall man of youthful appearance between them. Their arms were locked, and each seemed to be steadying the other. The band burst forth with loud music.

As they passed me I saw the man in the middle shake his head, and say, "Too loud." He beckoned for a bell boy, and handed him a hundred dollar bill.

"Give the band leader that, and tell him he's making too much noise. Tell him to play something soft." He gave the boy a five dollar tip.

Soft music prevailed during the rest of the evening.

Charlie enjoyed the fair. The commissioners enjoyed him. Hugh Campbell and Shirley Christy were experienced and devoted poker players. So was their guest. They had some exciting games. Double eagles were used as chips. Though Charlie was said to like thousand dollar antes he didn't take advantage of the country boys; in fact, from what I gathered later, the natives took Charlie for seven thousand dollars. That didn't mean anything to one who had often sat in games with tens of thousands on the table. A poker playing friend sent Charlie a newspaper clipping which mentioned a game in which he had participated that had a million dollars on the table. In replying Charlie said that as he remembered it the amount had been four million. I felt that he was joking, but I was never sure.

Four years later I was to meet Charlie Clark in his office at the United Verde Copper Company at Jerome, to have him decide whether or not a native farm boy was capable of retaining employment as secretary to the assistant general manager, Will L. Clark, and of serving Charlie himself on his Jerome trips as a stenographer and office assistant. Characteristically, Will L. had left this decision to Charlie; he had been disappointed that I didn't have a college degree and would not employ such a man in a position of that importance without his superior's approval.

Like the town he bossed, Charles Walker Clark, eldest son of William Andrews Clark, appeared on the surface to have many characters. He could be austere and cordial, arrogant and friendly, rough and polished, domi-neering and warm, kind and cruel, generous and miserly; which character-istic dominated depended upon his mood or his like or dislike of the per-son in contact. In Jerome he was known as a good executive, friendly to the company's employees, a good drinker and card player, and quite a hand with the ladies.

One old timer well expressed the effect a visit from Charlie Clark had on Jerome. "Everybody was happy when Charlie came to town. He had lots of money. He gave money to a lot of people. He would stay in the Fashion saloon all night, playing poker and doing other things."

Charles Walker Clark was born in 1871 in Deer Lodge. By the time he was old enough to attend school his father had become the wealthiest man in Montana, and with unlimited means he planned that his children should have the best of everything, including education at schools of such prominence that they would gain prestige and an entrance into society. Charlie's initial education was under private tutors, both at home and in Europe. He then attended prep schools in New York and in 1889 entered Yale.

He had a keen mind, but he enjoyed social affairs and sports, and he did not tie himself to text books beyond the point of obtaining passable grades. His father made him substantial allowances, but Charlie even then was becoming a heavy spender and frequently spent beyond his income. He told Tom Campbell of an occasion when his father decided to come up to New Haven to investigate personally the reason for Charlie's request for an increased allowance. This posed something of a problem; his money had been spent on gambling and girls, and there was nothing tangible to show for the dissolution of his generous remittances. But he found a solution.

Charlie had a classmate who was the owner of some good paintings. He borrowed some of these and hung them in his own quarters. When his father arrived Charlie proudly claimed the paintings as his own, and gave a discourse on art and its importance to humanity; he told of the inspira-tion the paintings were giving him, and strongly urged his sire to purchase fine works by the masters and become uplifted too. The old man, said Charlie, was tremendously impressed by his son's appreciation for the finer things in life, and shelled out the funds required for Charlie's immediate needs and increased his allowance. Further, Charlie boasted, his father took his advice, began to take an interest in the works of the masters, and eventually acquired the collection which cost him millions.

While Charlie thus had found knowledge of art useful, he didn't pursue it. He did develop a liking for rare books, and became well known as a collector of incunabula and first editions.

Following his graduation from Yale Charlie returned to Butte, and at his father's urging began to learn the rudiments of the mining and smelting business. When the smelter was built at Jerome he was sent down there to make himself familiar with the mine and smelter and to prepare himself for taking a hand in the United Verde's management.

In 1896 he was married to Katherine Roberts, who died in 1904. There were no children by this marriage.

Charlie took a keen interest in Montana politics, and became his father's right hand man in his political manipulations. Mainly he worked behind the scenes, directing others and supplying money.

Following the notorious campaign which culminated in William A. Clark's first election to the United States Senate in 1900, the only official charge brought against the Clark organization was directed at a Clark attorney, who was disbarred in punishment. Charles escaped indictment then, and even though it was a near miss he didn't learn much of caution from the experience.

Charlie helped in the 1901 campaign which resulted in the seating of his father in the Senate the following year.

At that time the Senator was opposing F. Augustus Heinze, and Charlie got into the war of the copper kings. He was accused of endeavoring to bribe a judge by offering him a quarter of a million dollars to admit that his decision in a mining case which had been decided in favor of Heinze and against the Amalgamated Copper Company, had been influenced by a payment to him by Heinze. The effort failed, and a charge of attempted bribery was filed against Charles W. Clark.

Charlie fled and took up residence in California. The indictment remained alive for many years, and during that period Charlie supposedly did not dare set foot in Montana. He did return once, though. I remember the highly secret preparations that were made during a period when Charlie was in Jerome to enable him to cross the Idaho-Montana border at a remote point to sign some papers which required attestation in Montana. This done he quickly retreated. Once later he returned to his native state, after the indictment had finally become void; that was on business in connection with the sale of the Clark interests in Montana to the

Anaconda Company after the Senator's death. After that he was through with his native state.

Charlie acquired an estate in San Mateo, where he lived with his wife until her death. Six months later, he married Celia Tobin, member of a prominent San Francisco banking family. There were three daughters by this marriage and a son who died in 1963. This match gave Charlie entry into California society. He acquired a string of racing horses, one of which he named "United Verde", but no dividends resulted. He played polo, and was admitted into various clubs.

His father made him general manager of the United Verde Copper Company, and he interspersed business with his pleasures by making frequent trips to Jerome. With the expansion of the company culminating in the building of the Clarkdale smelter, Charlie realized and convinced his aging father that larger authority must be granted the local executive, and he agreed with Robert E. Tally when the latter told him that he could not accept a subservient position such as his predecessor Will L. Clark had held, and that if he took the job he must be allowed to manage. Thus the United Verde in 1916 acquired its first resident manager with the authority to make important decisions.

Charlie like his father was a Francophile, and made frequent trips to Europe. He had a good time at the resorts and casinos with his male and female friends. His relations with his wife deteriorated, and shortly after the Senator's death in 1925 she agreed to a divorce. The settlement demanded and received, largely in trusts for the children, took away a substantial part of Charlie's assets, including a large portion of his United Verde shares and the San Mateo estate. Soon after this divorce he married Elizabeth Judge of Salt Lake City, and this union was preserved through the remaining years of Charlie's life.

Those last years were not particularly happy ones for Charlie Clark. His health had been undermined, some said by drinking; he died in 1933. He willed all he had left with the exception of a few small items to his widow, who two years later sold her United Verde shares to Phelps Dodge Corporation.

After the death of Charles Walker Clark I asked one who had been closely associated with him and his family if Charlie had accomplished anything at all of benefit to society.

"Yes," was the answer. "He fathered four fine children, three lovely daughters and a son."

THOMAS TAYLOR

The Man from Wales

THOMAS TAYLOR

One windy day in the late winter of 1931 Thomas Taylor, general superintendent of United Verde's Clarkdale smelter, asked me to step across the hall from my office to his and bring my notarial seal.

On his desk was a document the text of which he concealed by placing other papers upon it, but the glimpse I had of it showed it to be written in his own angular, slanting hand. Seated near his desk were Alvin L. Reese, the smelter's chief chemist, Charles W. Fairfield, Taylor's secretary, and Thomas B. Jones, Clarkdale merchant.

"I've written me up a will," Taylor announced. "These boys here will witness it, and I want it notarized too."

He dipped a pen and signed his name. The witnesses signed. I completed the jurat, not knowing that I was aiding in the completion of a document that, less than two years later, was to receive publicity from one end of the country to the other.

On November 22, 1932, an obituary notice was flashed over news service wires. Part of it follows:

"Thomas Taylor, one of the most colorful figures in the history of mining in the West, died today at the United Verde hospital in Jerome at the age of 67. His death followed a self-inflicted bullet wound . . .

"Mr. Taylor had been in poor health for some months past, having undergone a series of mouth operations in New York . . . Worn down by suffering, and evidently in the fear it might be necessary for him to undergo further operations, he performed the act which ended in his death."

The name Tom Taylor was known throughout the smelting and mining industry of the West. He was praised by practical mining men who were proud that a man of limited education could have advanced so far. The graduate engineers acknowledged his ability as a practical smelterman even though, from the eminence of university degrees, they denied the knowledge of metallurgy which he claimed to have.

II. V. Smelter at Clarkdale as it appeared about the time of Thomas Taylor's death

BERTON F. YOUNG PHOTO

THE MAN FROM WALES

He was stockily built, with craggy features; a man of moods, often gruff, sometimes overbearing. After brief schooling he went to work as a water boy at a smelter in Swansea, Wales, where he was born in 1865. At the age of fourteen a brother-in-law brought him to America, where at Weir City, Kansas, he first found work. During the next three years he worked in the zinc smelters at Pittsburg, Kansas, and Joplin, Missouri, becoming at age seventeen one of the youngest furnacemen in the industry. But he could not forget the green hills of Wales and in 1882 returned to Swansea. He worked in the smelters there for a few years, during which time he acquired a wife and son. But again his feet began to itch and he worked his way back to America on a cattle boat.

Attracted to the booming copper camps of Montana, Taylor traveled to Great Falls, where he found employment in the smelter of the Boston and Montana company. There he began to show greater than average ability as a practical smelter man. Offered a position as shift boss in William A. Clark's Butte smelter, he performed so well that Clark sent him to Jerome when his new United Verde smelter was fired up in 1895. There under Superintendent Joseph L. Giroux he was made blast furnace foreman.

In 1898 Taylor fell victim to the gold fever which drew so many hundreds of men to Alaska and the Klondike. He did not find gold, but he found adventure which formed the basis for many a racy anecdote in his later years. He also found hardships beside which the rough living of the Western mining camps was a featherbed in a field of rocks. In 1900 he was back at his job in the Jerome smelter, and five years later he was appointed smelter superintendent.

In 1915, when the new smelter on the Verde was ready for operation, Taylor moved to Clarkdale and continued the job of bossing the operations, which in 1916 fell under the supervision of Robert E. Tally.

One of Tally's goals was to create, through the adoption of modern methods, the most efficient operation possible. He was loyal to the old timers, but began to bring in college men with up to date technical training in the more and more complicated metallurgical and mining problems.

Modern smelting, following the ever decreasing grade of ores, required intricate calculations to obtain the best smelting mixtures to bring about the highest possible extraction of copper. Taylor did not deny this, but he did deny that a college education could instill knowledge comparable to that gained by long years of experience. He tried without success to get

101

rid of a brilliant metallurgist who in later years went up the ladder to the highest position Phelps Dodge had to offer in its Western operations.

"I don't need figures to tell me how to smelt ore," he told me on one occasion. "We run smooth for a lot of years, didn't we? These damn pencil pushers should come to me for information, not try to teach me."

In 1925 Taylor was appointed general superintendent of the Clarkdale operations. He was told that this advancement was in appreciation for his long and loyal service, but with that tribute went the hint that he should let the technically trained engineers do the dirty work under his general command. He accepted the verdict with the help of an anodyne—a generous increase in salary. But he began to brood.

He would sit for long periods at his desk, pipe in mouth and a package of shag tobacco at hand. The higher officials of the company made much of him, which soothed but did not cure his darker moods. Then his vigor began to be sapped by the developing malignancy which was the underlying cause of his decision to take his life.

Tom Taylor was four times married. In addition to the son he left in Wales and who joined him in later years, in Montana a second wife gave him a daughter. In Jerome he married a widow with a daughter who married Tom's son. This marriage ended in divorce. His fourth marriage was to a woman he had known in earlier years in Montana, a widow with a son and a daughter who came to Clarkdale with her.

He was an acquistive man. He early determined to become wealthy, and if that required being called a miser, so be it. He bought and sold properties with acumen, and invested in good securities. He saved most of his generous salary, holding personal and household expenses to a minimum. No one but he knew the extent of his accumulations. After his death safety deposit boxes in Arizona and California were traced, stuffed with securities and cash, including gold, and there were rumours, probably groundless, that there were undiscovered treasures either in locked vaults or buried in the earth.

In his domestic relations Tom Taylor had many troubles. His last wife, like previous ones, incurred his displeasure, and in the broodings of his final years his feelings toward her became so bitter that he decided to punish her through provisions of his will.

What his secret testament provided no one guessed until it was read at a meeting of the executors with members of his family. To various blood relatives—a daughter, grandchildren, and nephews—he bequeathed a total of $45,000; to his wife $25,000; and to his son $125,000.

But a note to the executors in a closing paragraph of the will contained a bomb. They might wonder why he made the will the way he did, but he had good cause, he explained. He had made a previous will, but it was stolen from him; he was told it was destroyed, which was a lie. His wife and her daughter, he said, had done everything to get his money while he was alive; now he was leaving his wife enough to get them into HELL as soon as possible.

He concluded by saying that his wife had belittled him more than any human being ever did, "and I hope she and her daughter will pay for it when they get my money to go to HELL with."

The angry widow was preparing to contest the will when Robert E. Tally arranged a compromise between her and the son, whereby each was to receive approximately half of the $340,000 estate after all other bequests and expenses were taken care of. The two had approximately a quarter of a million dollars to divide.

Tom Taylor left many friends. They took him for what he was—a rough, unschooled product of early Western mining camps, who had few inhibitions and no fear of what others might think of him. In time this attitude built up for him a position which was unique, his alone in his own stamping ground—what Tom Taylor did that might have been condemned or ridiculed in others was accepted as part of the Tom Taylor tradition. His failings were outshadowed by his successes. Among his descendants his name will remain the bright and living legend of a poor boy from Wales who made good in a newer land across the seas.

Tom Taylor and unknown woman at the closing of the Jerome Smelter,
August 28, 1915. (Jerome Historical Society)

The Man from Colorado

WILL LEE CLARK

Will L. Clark peered at me through thick-lensed glasses, after I had taken my seat beside his desk, notebook ready. Open before him was the latest issue of the Jerome News.

"I see United Verde Extension is up to a dollar and a half," he observed. "They've found ore. I was sure they would."

A few moments was spent in silent musing.

"You know," he finally resumed, "when plans were first being made for the Hopewell tunnel [the tunnel driven from the thousand foot level to open on the hillside a mile eastward from the mine, to be used for drainage and waste haulage] I urged the Senator and C. W. to take an option on the UVX claims and drive the tunnel through them. They and the mine superintendent acted like I was crazy. 'No ore below the fault', they said. The claims would have cost only a quarter of a million. Look what they stand to lose. The stock's worth far more than that now, and it's going up. By the way, have you bought any?"

"No, sir. No money."

He slid open a drawer and took out a check book. He filled in a blank.

"Here's fifteen hundred dollars. Buy yourself a thousand shares. Write me a note if you want to. Pay me back when you like."

Will Lee Clark, who bore the title then of assistant general manager, was not a relative of William A. Clark. He was the first man aside from Charles W. Clark ever to have been granted a managerial title at the Jerome properties.

Born in Colorado in 1865, his final educational training was received at the Lowville Academy in New York. Subsequently, attracted by mining even though he had not studied mining or metallurgy, he took up residence in Butte. After a period of office work which placed him in contact with some men of influence, he received appointment as clerk of the superior court of Silver Bow county. There he became acquainted with the Clarks. He entered the Senator's employ as assistant business manager of one of his companies. Rumor had it that his transfer to Jerome in a responsible position was made in compensation for a service rendered in connection with a hush-hush matter in which one of the Clarks was involved. This came at a time when it had been decided to relieve H. J. Allen of his anomalous position with the United Verde, and Will L. was assigned to replace him.

Will Clark arrived in Jerome the day Allen committed suicide early in 1904. He was a man easily disturbed, and his predecessor's tragic death shocked and depressed him. This was a factor in an attitude toward his job which at times appeared to be timid. The Allen impact on the people of Jerome had been positive, if not popular, and this impress was long lasting. Will Clark strove for a popularity which, lacking a firm approach, he could not achieve.

He was further handicapped by the lofty bearing and aggressive attitude of his wife who, with an entire lack of foresight and tact, undertook to direct her husband in the management of the copper company. That Will L. did not forcibly resist this was one factor in the growing impatience general manager Charles W. Clark felt for him.

Will L. Clark was first appointed superintendent. In 1908 he was given the title of assistant general manager and in 1913 manager. But in line with the Senator's personal domination of all his enterprises, he was neither encouraged or allowed to make decisions of importance. He reported almost daily to the general manager, in long letters which in many instances were more in the nature of newsletters than official reports of operations. No internecine squabbles failed of detailed report. Decisions and settlements were left to Charles W., who had the responsibility of keeping the Senator informed of conditions in Arizona.

Will L. did not relish politics, nor was he by temperament or training the type from which a successful politician could be made. At any rate, the days of the political blunderbus and the bold approach with a stuffed sack was departing. Charles W., his lesson well learned in Montana, used as much finesse in his dealings as each situation demanded. The influencing of lawmakers was left to attorneys, professional agents, or the skilled representatives of the mine owners of the state who were beginning to unite and form their own protective associations.

Will L. Clark was an office man, and successful to the extent that he could analyze reports and make summations which were often the means by which Charles W. made decisions or recommendations to the Senator.

But in some respects he was considered a dreamer, as when he endeavored to combine the construction of the Hopewell tunnel with the prospecting of the UVX claims.

Will L. had the faith of his convictions, though; he began to buy UVX shares when Jim Douglas took over the UVX and commenced to explore. This foresight enabled him to retire a moderately wealthy man.

Will Clark remained with the United Verde twelve years. During this period the workings of the mine were extended. He predicted the value of the Hull claims and negotiated the million dollar deal through which the Hull claims were acquired.

Because of his success in the mining end of the business Tally's star had been rising, and concurrently Will L. Clark's restricted influence commenced a decline. Serious problems began to arise in the construction of the Clarkdale smelter with which he had difficulty in coping. T. C. ("Colonel") Roberts, the chief construction engineer on the project, was a driving but arrogant man who set his sights toward higher things. He impressed Charles Clark, but incurred the displeasure of Will L., Tally and Tom Taylor.

Will L. moved his office to Clarkdale in 1915, the year the new smelter was blown in. Roberts was then eyeing the manager's job and had reason to believe he would get it; he belittled Will L., refused to take orders from him, and in one case even issued an order that none of the company cars, including the manager's, could be taken from the plant without a pass from him. Such acts as this were considered by Will L. as insulting to his position, but he was forced to take the matter to Charles Clark before the order was rescinded.

Because of such harrassments, and the realization that others too were showing less than full respect for his position, Will L. began to feel that his resignation must be inevitable.

The Green Monster affair was to be one of the main factors in this decision. Will L. was part owner of a group of mining claims near Jerome, and when the big boom commencing with the United Verde Extension's bonanza discovery in 1915 was under way he and a few associates conceived the idea of forming a company to work the claims, which had indications of ore. He asked Charles Clark if the United Verde officials would object to his joining in a development project. Charles said they would not, whereupon the Green Monster Mining Company was organized and its shares placed on the market.

Promotion stock was offered at twenty-five cents, but for this stock offering, the first of many offerings of boom companies which sprouted in every direction, such a tremendous demand developed that the shares were raised to seventy-five cents. At the height of the boom five dollars was bid for Green Monster. The success of the UVX had inflamed the imagination of the speculating public, which was ready to grab at anything with a Jerome tag to it.

Will L. Clark was president of the Green Monster, and because of the similarity of his name to that of the Senator it became linked in the public mind with that of William A. Clark, to the annoyance of Charles and his father. Ignoring the fact that he had raised no objection to Will L. joining the Green Monster venture, he was blamed and censured to his deep resentment.

The sale of the shares had provided the Green Monster with a fat treasury. A development was started. Will L. could have sold the shares he had received for his interest in the property for enough to have made him rich, but he refused to do this. Others in the company were not so conscientious. They profited, and also, eyeing the money in the treasury, fought Will L.'s insistence that the money must be used for development. In the proxy fight which ensued he was ousted from the presidency and directorate. The victors took the offices, placed themselves on salaries while letting development dawdle, and drained the treasury dry.

Will L. Clark resigned his position with the United Verde, but one of his last and most vigorous acts was to urge the appointment of Robert E. Tally as his successor instead of T. C. Roberts, who had seemed to have the inside track. Charles and the Senator listened, and after investigating the relative popularity and abilities of the two candidates chose Tally.

Will L. tried to recover his control of the Green Monster, but the men at the trough had too much at stake to permit it.

When the United States declared war against Germany in World War I Will L. Clark was appointed by his friend Governor Thomas E. Campbell as state fuel administrator. At war's end he took up residence in California. He continued his interest in mining, and during the thirties and early forties owned and operated a small mine, with brief residences in Colorado and Nebraska. He died in Los Angeles in 1951 at the age of 86.

While Arthur Train, Jr., was collecting information for a history of Phelps Dodge Corporation, he interviewed a person whose name was prominent in Arizona — one who had attained some fame in the literary

eld and who had held a state post under a governor's appointment. Asked
bout Will L., even though this person's acquaintance with him had not
een close a positive though reckless judgment was quickly delivered!

"He would have made a good tin horn. He didn't know what honesty
eant."

Will L. Clark didn't deserve such a condemnation. He was a conscien-
ous executive within the limits of his ability and the barriers erected by
is dominating employers. He was honorable in his personal dealings and
ady to offer aid to those who needed help.

Were I to write an epitaph for Will L. Clark it would be:

"He was an honest man, and did the best he could."

Robert E. Tally

The Man from Nevada

ROBERT EMMET TALLY

Neither Bob Tally nor his partner Ernest Fredell were feeling any too good that morning. They had been out a little too late the night before, and they hated to leave the balmy spring air and sunshine for the dank and chilly drift they were timbering in the Golden Hunter mine at Mullen, Idaho. They found the shift boss ahead of them, inspecting the last timbers which had been set by the graveyard shift.

Tally joined in the inspection.

"Sloppy," he volunteered. "The caps and girts fit bad."

"Good enough. These timbermen ain't cabinet makers."

Tally made an uncomplimentary remark which aroused the shift boss's ire.

"Too much college," he sneered. "You don't learn how to do real work there — just to find fault."

"Too bad you never went to school," Tally retorted.

"I know more about mining than you'll ever know. I've had a belly full of you damn slide rule swellheads."

Sticking his chin out, the shift boss glared up into the young man's face. It was too good a target to ignore. Tally swung and connected. The shift boss hit the dirt, and before he could regain his feet Tally turned toward the shaft.

"I've had enough of Idaho, anyway," he said to Fredell. "Think I'll go to Montana. Want to go along?"

The two left Mullen and went to Butte. They had no idea of it then, but both were to end their travels at the United Verde down in Arizona.

Robert Emmet Tally was born in Virginia City, Nevada, in 1877, the son of Thomas and Jane Tally, Irish immigrants. The father worked as a miner on the Comstock lode, and reached a foreman's status.

Bob attended the Nevada School of Mines and was graduated in 1899 with the degrees of Bachelor of Science and Mining Engineer. He worked as a miner in Nevada, British Columbia, and Idaho, looking for oppor-

111

tunities. He found them when he was employed in the mines of Senator Clark in Butte. There was room to grow there.

The Senator was always on the alert for bright young men with technical training, and at this time he wanted someone to go down to Arizona. His attention was called to the man from Nevada. Tally looked and acted like he might fill the bill, and he was sent to Jerome. He familiarized himself with the underground conditions and ore deposits by working as a miner. It was not long before he was made a shift boss, and then a foreman. In 1908 he was appointed mine superintendent. He was made assistant general manager upon Will L. Clark's resignation in 1916.

Fredell too was sent to Jerome by Senator Clark, to become chief electrical engineer of the mines department.

I well remember the first meeting Tally called of the heads of departments after he had taken the manager's chair. "There has been too much quarrelling and fighting in this organization," he told the men. "It's going to stop. Now you have three choices, and only three: Cooperate — or quit, or get fired."

The Clarkdale smelter had been operating for a year, but construction on various installations had been continuing in charge of "Colonel" Roberts. He had received some encouragement from Charles W. Clark in his ambition to take over management of the United Verde. He had made all arrangements to move into the executive office as soon as Will L. Clark left, and was planning changes in the mine and smelter staffs. After Tally took over it appeared to him that Roberts' attitude was such that full cooperation could not be expected, for he had received the news of the mine superintendent's promotion with white faced anger, followed by sullenness. It was not long afterward that Roberts was handed a letter from Charles W. Clark terminating his employment.

Fighting and bickering stopped, and the United Verde became a smooth running operation.

During World War I labor troubles developed. The miners' union called a strike over wages and working conditions, which Tally successfully settled. Then the Industrial Workers of the World, red dominated, attempted to take over labor leadership in Jerome and Clarkdale; though they had only a hundred members they did manage to halt operations. With Tally's encouragement a citizens' "committee" rounded up the "Wobblies", loaded them in cattle cars, and shipped them out. On the main line they sent them west, but California refused to let them enter that state. They were finally turned loose at Kingman, but Jerome was bothered with Wobblies no more during the war.

Bisbee was having Wobbly trouble too, on a larger scale. They took Jerome's example, and Cochise County offiicials and citizens shipped out a thousand of the I.W.W., invoking "the law of necessity" which became a famous issue in connection with the lawsuits which resulted from the deportation.

In 1921 Charles W. Clark relinquished the title of general manager to Tally, who had built up a solid organization. He was good at picking men. Many who got their start with the United Verde went on to high positions with other companies. United Verde trained men were in demand. Tally himself could have taken other high positions — in one instance after the Senator's death he was offered the presidency of a vigorous young exploration company, together with stock options which alone would have made him a millionaire. But he was loyal to the Senator and Charles W. Clark, who had given him his chance. At that time the Senator's daughters had begun to make dissension, and Tally felt he could be of help as a mediator, a role which time after time he was called upon to fill.

As he was loyal himself, he demanded loyalty of others. This was his cult. To remain in the company's employ one had to be a company man without equivocation. Also he expected loyalty from those the company supported in politics or business. To those who fought him or his company he could be ruthless.

The third decade of the century was a busy time for Tally. He was active in a number of organizations, industrial and civic. He was president of the American Institute of Mining and Metallurgical Engineers, and of the American Mining Congress, and became one of the best known men in the mining world. The United Verde prospered enormously. The open pit produced cheap ores in quantity; the Clarkdale smelter capacity was increased and produced up to fifteen million pounds of copper per month. The company shared its income to some extent by paying high salaries and making life comfortable and entertaining for the employees, providing club houses, a golf course, tennis courts, baseball fields, swimming pools, libraries, picnic and play grounds, and parks.

Tally prospered personally through speculations in the stock market. Starting with a sizeable block of UVX shares he ran up a fortune of well over a million dollars. He liked to take chances; he failed to heed warning signs prior to the crash of 1929, with the result that his fortune was almost wiped out.

The United Verde mine and smelter continued to operate into 1931, but with no market for copper — and quotations down to five cents a pound — it eventually had to close, not to open again until 1935.

Ever see an acre of copper — or one, or two, or three acres of copper bars, stacked on edge? That's what there was in the Clarkdale yards. Ninety million pounds of it — 300,000 bars. Phelps Dodge got it when they took over United Verde in 1935.

After the Senator's death in 1925 the contest between his sons and daughters for control of the company became more and more bitter. But Charles was chosen president of the United Verde, and soothed by high dividends matters were comparatively quiet until the financial disaster of 1929. Then things really began to unravel.

Charles W. Clark left the presidency to go upstairs to board chairman, and Tally was elected president. He exerted strenuous efforts to bring peace, but did not succeed. The sisters felt the men of their families should have had a more prominent part in the operation of the company, and jealousies persisted. Control of the company rested with the owners of one or two minority blocks of stock; so far these had been voted for the brothers, but the sisters continued to scheme and hope.

When Tally took the president's chair and established residence in New York, W. Val DeCamp was appointed general manager. DeCamp had become mine superintendent when his predecessor, H. DeWitt Smith, took an important position with Newmont Mining Company. While he had years of mining experience he had no particular sense of loyalty or gratitude toward those who had given him his opportunities. He had a devious mind and liked intrigue, in which he was frequently involved within the organization. During the depression when the battle between the heirs had reached its height and the balance of power was teetering, DeCamp had contact with the sisters, who expected to make a house cleaning and appoint a manager and other officers who had no such stubborn fidelities as had Tally.

DeCamp was very receptive to this approach. He began to line up a proposed executive staff, which contemplated the firing of most of the Tally men. He informed intimates that he would remain loyal to the Clark brothers and Tally as long as it appeared they would remain in power, but he intended to do what was best for himself. Charles W.

Clark and Tally learned of this, and when the voting at the next annual election proved to be in their favor DeCamp was fired.

In 1931 William A. Clark Junior's son, William A. Clark III, called Tertius, came to Clarkdale. He had some technical training and was anxious to join the United Verde staff. Tally encouraged him, and suggested various assignments whereby he could study the United Verde operation and the metals industries in general. Tertius took up this work enthusiastically. He had United Verde shares his father had given him, and the thought began to develop among members of the company staff that Tertius might be the man eventually to bring the opposing forces together. That hope vanished when he was killed in an airplane crash while piloting one of his planes on a Sunday flight in 1932. Killed with him was Jack Lynch, employed by Tertius as pilot and director of an air school he was developing. Lynch had been one of Lindbergh's instructors.

In 1932 Tally organized the Arizona Emergency Council. One of the principal objects of the council was to find sources of revenue other than the ad valorem tax in order to relieve the harried property owners of the burden of furnishing the major part of the support for state, county and municipal governments. In this organization a plan for a privilege sales tax was worked out. The plan appealed to Governor B. B. Moeur, who incorporated it into his program, and his legislature enacted it into law.

After Phelps Dodge Corporation acquired control of the United Verde in 1935 Tally returned to Arizona. His close friend Louis S. Cates was then president of Phelps Dodge, and as Tally's pride would not permit him to remain as a mere branch manager, as he was asked to do, he retired to private life. Soon afterward he developed the malady which caused his death in 1936.

Robert Emmett Tally was twice married; first in Montana, where a son and a daughter were born; second, in Jerome, a union which brought another son.

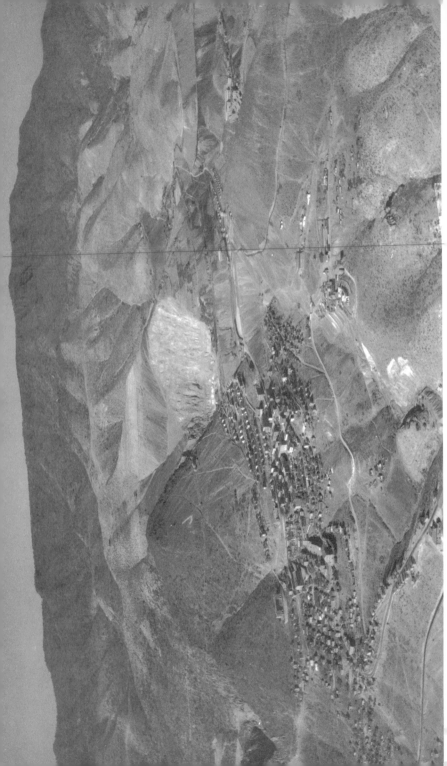

Aerial view of Clarkdale today, showing remnants of smelter. Cement plant is at left center.

Dr. James Douglas

James S. Douglas

Lewis W. Douglas

Father, Son and Grandson
THE DOUGLAS FAMILY

The greatest impact upon Jerome of the Douglas name was made at a time when the expansion of the United Verde Copper Company's mines and reduction plants was nearing its height, though twice before one member of the Douglas line had taken a hand in United Verde dealings.

It was a son of James Douglas Jr. who took over the development of a group of claims which Senator Clark and well known geologists had scorned, and discovered ore deposits of bonanza proportions, setting off the greatest mining boom that twentieth century Arizona has known. This was James Stuart Douglas, popularly known as "Rawhide Jimmy".

Actually, James S. Douglas was a third generation scion of a line which had an active interest in mining. His grandfather, Dr. James Douglas, was a physician of Scottish birth, a member of the Royal College of Surgeons, who came to America and established a practice in Utica, New York. Subsequently he moved to Quebec and became a renowned surgeon there, and because of a deep concern for the unfortunate he founded the Quebec Insane Asylum and directed it for some years.

Previous activities included service as ship's doctor on a whaling vessel and physician to a colonization group in Nicaragua.

As further indication of a venturesome spirit, Dr. Douglas invested in a number of mining ventures, none of which proved successful and which finally caused his financial downfall.

James Douglas, Junior — also Doctor by reason of degrees in the field of science but commonly known as "Professor"— was born in Quebec in 1837, the only one of four sons to reach maturity. At the age of eighteen years, with family encouragement, he decided to enter the Presbyterian ministry. He entered Edinburgh University, only to be called back to Quebec because of the illness to his mother which resulted in her death. He then studied for two years in Queen's College in Kingston, Ontario, followed by two more years of theological studies at Edinburgh. Before time for ordination he fought a battle with his conscience which resulted in the decision that he could not sign the required confession of faith. He was, and remained, a good Christian, but he had developed an opposition to strict denominationalism.

While in Edinburgh he met and married Naomi Douglas, whose father was commodore captain and superintendent of construction of the Cunard line. Though of the same name they were not related.

After the decision to discontinue theological study James Douglas Jr. returned to Quebec and worked with his father in his enterprises. Concurrently he took up the study of medicine at Laval University. He left Quebec to try to salvage a mine in which his father had a heavy investment, an endeavor which failed. By then the elder Douglas had become so involved in his various ventures he was in deep financial trouble.

While at Laval James Junior had formed a friendship with Thomas Sterry Hunt, a professor of chemistry and one of his instructors, who had been head of the Canadian Geological Survey. Together they worked out a new method of extracting copper from low grade ores by leaching, which became known as the Hunt and Douglas process. Their mutual research led to the establishment of the first plant in America for the electrolytic refining of copper.

They assisted in the organization of the Chemical Copper Company, their plant being set up at Phoenixville, Pennsylvania. James Junior was named superintendent. With his aging father's fortune gone, in 1875 the Quebec home was sold, and all other family possessions were disposed of in an effort to liquidate the debts. The Douglas home was re-established in Pennsylvania.

The ores from the Pennsylvania mines were not rich enough to make the Phoenixville operation a success financially, and additional metals from custom sources were sought. In 1880 Douglas traveled to Arizona to consult with officials of the Copper Queen mine regarding the refining of their copper. It was on this trip that James Douglas Jr. traveled up to the Black Hills mines by stage and horseback to negotiate the option on the Eureka and Wade Hampton claims for Logan and Lennig.

He was subsequently engaged by Phelps, Dodge & Company in a consulting capacity, and through his recommendations Phelps, Dodge became interested financially in the Copper Queen and other mines in Arizona. Taking part of his compensation in shares, and directing the development of the Copper Queen and its subsidiary mines, in the face of hardships and at times near financial collapse, James Douglas Jr. eventually achieved wealth, the presidency of Phelps, Dodge and Company, and a high position in American mining. He died in 1918 at the age of eighty-one.

James Stuart Douglas, the "Rawhide Jimmy" of Southwestern fame, was born in Quebec in 1867. He was seven years of age when his family moved to Pennsylvania. He was of an independent and aggressive nature; because of his family's financial straits he set out on his own when only seventeen years of age. Because of an asthmatic condition he took his doctor's advice and traveled west to Manitoba in search of relief. He worked for wages, driving a team and fresno scraper on the construction of the Canadian National Railroad.

He filed on a homestead and operated it for a number of years. At age twenty-two he went to Arizona and tried to raise strawberries in the Sulphur Springs Valley in Cochise County. Discovering the enterprise to be unpromising, he took employment in an assay office in Bisbee. Later he went to northern Arizona for Phelps Dodge to manage the Commercial mine near Prescott. He also had charge of the Senator and Big Bug mines. Here he first came in contact and gained knowledge of the Jerome district.

In 1900 he returned to Bisbee. Knowing that a new smelter for the treatment of Copper Queen and custom ores would eventually be built, he and some prominent associates bought land in the Sulphur Springs Valley a few miles from the Bisbee mines, and laid out a townsite which was named Douglas in honor of his father. Lots were sold, utilities established, and business buildings constructed. He helped organize the Bank of Douglas and the Bank of Bisbee.

James S. Douglas made money. He was not afraid to venture. One acquaintance said of him, "When he won, he won big. If he made a bust, it would be a big bust," But the wins exceeded the busts.

He married Josephine Williams, daughter of Lewis Williams of Bisbee, one of the developers of the Copper Queen. He became an American citizen.

While the town of Douglas was being developed James S. returned to mining. In 1900 he went to Sonora, Mexico, and took management of the Moctezuma Copper Company's mine at Pilares and their smelter at Nacozari, and directed the building of a railroad from Douglas.

Later he took the management of the Cananea Copper Company. In

The United Verde Extension Mine and Daisy Hotel.

The U.V.X. Mine, c. 1920, with Clarkdale town and smelter in the distance.

the Cananea mines Americans were mainly employed. He replaced most of these with native workmen, believing that Mexicans should be engaged in the development of their own resources. In spite of this action, agitators promoted trouble. There was rioting, and it was demanded that James S. get out, and the Mexican military commander advised him to. He did leave but was back in three days.

Economies were effected at Cananea which increased the earnings of the company. Economies were needed in the New York office too, James S. believed, and he tried to bring them about. This met with resistance, and he resigned.

A number of versions regarding the origin of the name "Rawhide Jimmy" have been circulated. Cleland in his history of Phelps Dodge states that the name originated at Nacozari when James S. used rawhide to protect the rollers of an incline to prevent their damage by the cables. Another story is that he was so named because he was rough, tough, and "rawhided" the men under him to unusual effort. Regarding this Lewis W. Douglas advised this writer as follows:

"The Cleland story is correct. The other legends are completely wrong. My father had a very powerful personality but he was kindly and thousands of people in Arizona owe their fortunes to his consideration of them. He combined in a very curious way the strength of a liberal with the common sense and penetrating capacity of a successful business man."

In 1912 James S. Douglas undertook his greatest venture, which became his most successful and which brought riches even beyond his hopes and profits to thousands of others.

As has been related in the chapter on George W. Hull, the United Verde Extension Gold, Silver & Copper Mining Company, called the UVX, had been organized by Hull in 1899. Lying between the group of claims included in the company's property and the United Verde was the Little Daisy, a fractional claim located by J. J. Fisher, a deputy United States mineral surveyor who discovered the unlocated ground while mapping the area. A promotion was started and a shaft sunk on the fraction. It then appeared that the best chance of finding ore lay in the Hull claims; a consolidation was effected, Hull trading the UVX claims for shares in the company.

The enterprise progressed through a reorganization and financing, in the process of which Hull traded his shares for full ownership of some of the company's outlying claims, until Major A. J. Pickrell, then the holder of a substantial block of UVX shares, interested James S. Douglas, who took an option on the company's property.

Lewis Douglas gives the following account of subsequent developments:

"My father offered the original option on the UVX to Phelps Dodge, who turned it down on the grounds that Senator Clark, who owned the United Verde, would have the apex on any ore found in UVX ground. Thereupon, together with George E. Tener, he undertook the development of the UVX. The original sum raised by my father and Mr. Tener was $250,000. . . . Additional finances were raised through underwriting by James S. Douglas and George E. Tener."

There were many disappointments, but through it all James S. and his associates retained their faith in the property. In December, 1914, a drift cut a deposit of 45 per cent copper ore. Further development disclosed other rich ores. A smelter was built in the valley. By the time the mine and smelter produced and treated all the ores of commercial value that could be found and closed in 1938, the UVX had paid $55,000,000 in dividends.

Through the development period of the UVX there was no promotion in the ordinary sense. Prospective buyers and stockholders were carefully informed that the venture was a speculation. They were told of the failures as well as the successes. While the shares were advancing from fifty cents to more than fifty dollars, James S. Douglas and his associates held their shares, and they held them still when the mine was worked out and closed. The dividends were their only profits.

In the first world war James S. was director of the warehouse division of the American Red Cross in France. He became an admirer and a friend of Georges Clemenceau, and named his smelter town for him.

During World War II James Stuart Douglas retired to his native land and resumed Canadian citizenship. There he died in 1949.

A fourth generation Douglas began in Jerome a distinguished career in politics, education, diplomacy and business.

This is Lewis Williams Douglas, elder son of James S. He was born in Bisbee in 1894. After graduating from Amherst College he enrolled in the Massachusetts Institute of Technology, leaving there to volunteer for military service in 1917 when the United States entered World War I. He served with distinction overseas as a lieutenant of field artillery, and received a citation from General Pershing. He also received the Belgian Croix de Guerre.

After the war he went to Jerome to work with his father in the United Verde Extension mine. He was keenly interested in mining and geology, an interest which he still retains, and with an associate developed, patented and successfully used in Alaska a process for the recovery of oxidized lead and silver ores.

In 1921 he married Peggy Zinsser, daughter of a well known New York family, whom he had met while a student at Amherst, and brought her to Jerome. His copper roofed home, built by his father as a wedding gift for him and his bride, is a structure of particular interest to visitors to the ghost city. To Lewis Douglas and his wife were born three children, James Stuart II, Lewis Williams Junior, and a daughter Sharman.

A keen interest in public affairs and government led Lewis Douglas in 1922 to enter politics. He became a successful candidate for election to the Arizona legislature's lower house. In 1926 he was sent to Washington as Arizona's sole member of the House of Representatives. He was serving his fourth term when he resigned to become Franklin D. Roosevelt's director of the budget. He held that post for eighteen months, then resigned because of a conviction that the program which the President was pursuing would make extravagant spending inevitable.

Prior to World War II President Roosevelt asked him to serve as a deputy war shipping administrator to allocate tonnage to the military and various civil programs and to serve on the combined shipping administration board. He accepted the post, and participated in conferences of the combined chiefs. After the war he was advisor to the control council which included Generals Eisenhower and Clay, and disagreed with the withdrawal of United States troops to their zones in the spring of 1945.

He was offered and declined the presidency of the World Bank.

In 1947 President Truman appointed him Ambassador to the Court of St. James's, where he gave the United States distinguished service. His impact and that of his family on the people of England is history.

In the field of education, after World War I he taught at Amherst, and later was principal of McGill University in Montreal, the only United States citizen to have so served.

In the business field he served for many years as president and chairman of the board of the Mutual Life Insurance Company of New York, and held official positions and directorates in a number of corporations.

After resigning his ambassadorship Lewis Douglas returned to Arizona, but not to a life of leisure. He operates a large ranch at Sonoita, near Tucson, where he has his office. He has banking and other business interests; he is active in public welfare work. His knowledge and talents have been on call whenever needed in the service of his country, his state and his community.

DON BARROWS PHOTO

Gutted shell of U.V.X. Daisy Hotel — 1964

The Douglas Mansion, now a museum of the Arizona Parks Board

JAMES FRANKLIN ROBERTS

Lawman from Missouri

JAMES FRANKLIN ROBERTS

The sun had long since dropped behind Cleopatra Hill, bringing early dusk to Jerome even while the rim of the Mogollons far to the east was still bathed in golden light.

Chief deputy Jim Roberts unlocked his post office box and removed his afternoon mail. There was a letter from the sheriff at Prescott. Though Jim was an unusually silent man he muttered a profane word as he read.

The board of supervisors had appropriated three hundred dollars to build a jail at Jerome. Lumber had been bought and would be shipped by wagon team.

Three hundred dollars for a jail to hold the toughs he had to run in? Jim snorted. What would he do for labor? Probably have to arrest himself some drunks and work them. But what kind of a jail would he have when they got through? Not much better than having his arrests shackled to hitching rails and wagon wheels, like now. Three hundred dollars. Hell.

Jim strolled down Main Street. In a vacant lot down street from the Fashion saloon a wagon had been left while a split tongue was being ironed. Handcuffed to a spoke on a front wheel was Dud Crocker, who had started a fight in a saloon and had to be pistol whipped by Deputy Joe Hawkins. The prisoner appeared to be asleep.

Roberts resumed his beat, paying no attention to Sid Chew loitering across the street. He checked the doors of the stores which were being closed for the night. Dusk was near.

Crocker wasn't asleep, but he kept on pretending as Roberts passed by on his way back up town. When he was gone Sid Chew hurried across the rutted, unpaved street, took a wrench from the tool box at the front of the wagon bed, and loosened the axle nut of the wheel to which Crocker was handcuffed. Then, hearing voices approaching, he walked casually away.

"Be back," he muttered.

Crocker was sobering, but he pretended a drunken slumber when

Hawkins passed by half an hour later and poked him with his toe. The man's hatred of Hawkins grew. He had been on his tail for a week and when he told the deputy to get the hell off his back or else, he had been gun whipped. He'd killed another man for less than that. He'd kill Hawkins.

It was dark when Chew returned, and the only activity was up in the saloons. Crocker had already finished unscrewing the axle nut. Chew jerked the wheel from the spindle, letting the greasy cone drop into the dirt. The two of them then picked up the heavy wheel, and carried it down the nearby side street to Hull Avenue and up to the door of a blacksmith shop.

With a pinch bar Chew had taken from the wagon he pried away the padlock which secured the pair of wide swinging doors. Inside he struck a match and found a coal oil lantern. While lighting it a voice at the rear of the shop shouted a query.

"Just a little job," Crocker answered. "Come out and help."

As a man stepped forward into the light he was recognized as the blacksmith's helper, who bunked in a storage room at the back. When he had come close Chew delivered a vicious blow to his jaw. As the man dropped he struck his head against the corner of an anvil. He was found dead next morning.

Chew found a chisel and hammer and cut the handcuffs from the wheel, then removed the cuff from Crocker's wrist. They doused the light, and hurried south a few doors to the boarding house where the men shared a room. A full moon was appearing over the eastern rim of the valley.

"What you figurin' now?" Chew asked.

"Kill Hawkins first, then get out of town. You with me?"

"It's Roberts I want," Chew replied. "I told him I'd get him after he split my scalp."

Each man took a pistol from the old chest of drawers and slipped it in his belt. They went out on the dark porch.

A sound of shouting came from up Main Street way. The escape had been discovered. Hawkins came running toward them. Knowing where Crocker lived he headed straight for the boarding house. Both Crocker and Chew started shooting. Hawkins returned the fire, wounding Chew slightly in the thigh. In the darkness of the porch the fugitives had the advantage. Hawkins fell dead.

LAWMAN FROM MISSOURI

Jim Roberts had gone home to get some sleep, but the two men knew it wouldn't be long until he would be on their trail. Crocker and Chew ran to the livery stable down at the bend of the valley road, and at gun point ordered the night man to saddle up two horses. They headed down the hill. The stableman rushed away to find Roberts, who already had been summoned.

Learning at the stable the direction Crocker and Chew had gone, Roberts saddled his favorite riding animal, a big white mule; especially at night he could trust the sure feet of this ungainly hybrid. He led a smaller mule carrying a pack saddle.

Over in Pleasant Valley, before the Graham gang stole his horses and shot his best pals, Jims Roberts had learned the fine points of trailing; but just trailing was too slow, especially at night. If you could outthink a man, though, you could save a lot of time. What would he do if he was on the run? There was only one way to get out of this part of the valley and lose a trail, and that was down river. He would take to the water. That would slow him up a lot, so he couldn't get past Camp Verde before morning. So he'd hole up for the day in the river groves and plan to by-pass Camp Verde the following night. This was what Crocker and Chew would probably do too, Jim reckoned. They'd hide at dawn, and they'd pick a spot with a hill nearby so they could scout the surrounding country.

Jim kept to the road, only once dismounting to look for fresh tracks. The bright moonlight showed him none. Yes, they'd be ridin' in the water.

He was in Camp Verde before morning, and learned from the deputy there that no riders had been seen. He took a ranch road back up river. When he approached a sizeable hill near the stream bed he left his animals; day was breaking when he climbed the slope, keeping a brush cover between him and the river. Carefully he watched. He wasn't surprised when he saw a thin thread of smoke rising from a thicket of lush watermoties.

Half an hour later Jim crawled up to where he could see Crocker and Chew crouched before a little fire, working the chill of out of their hands.

"No need of shootin'," Roberts called. "Just drop your guns. Don't draw."

The two men ignored the order. They sprang to their feet, separating, and began firing in the direction of the voice. Jim didn't hurry; no use wastin' bullets. He shot Crocker through the head. Chew spotted him by the shot, and came dodging toward him, spraying bullets. Jim dropped him.

Jerome's chief deputy rode into town that afternoon with the two killers roped to the pack mule. He delivered the bodies to the undertaker. He wired the sheriff at Prescott to send him another deputy.

That was one of the more active days in the life of the mild eyed, silent law man from Missouri. I have listened to many such stories told by old timers about Jim Roberts, all telling of the way he kept peace in the early days of Jerome. Through all of them has run a note of awe, and pride too — pride that the narrators had lived in Jerome when Jim Roberts was on the job.

James Franklin Roberts was a peace officer during a large part of the last forty years of his life. Though he took time off to do some ranching and prospecting, he always returned to his profession of keeping the peace. He served Jerome for a dozen years, first as deputy and constable, then as the elected town marshal after Jerome's incorporation as a town.

He was born in Bevier, Macon County, Missouri, in 1858. In early manhood he drifted westward to search for a country wild enough to suit an adventurous nature. He found what he was looking for up near the head of Tonto Creek under the Mogollon Rim in east central Arizona, in what came to be known as Pleasant Valley. This was in the heart of what was then one of the wildest sections of the American West.

Jim built a cabin and took up a profession he knew something about, the breeding of horses of class and stamina. He acquired brood mares and a fine stallion in which he took particular pride.

While Jim Roberts sought the wild country because it appealed to his nature, others sought if for different reasons. The law was moving westward, and outlaws and gunmen of the border and Rocky Mountain areas were searching for such a place as the wilderness under the rim. Many became connected with outlying ranches such as the Hashknife from which they could best retreat to the wild country if the law became too bothersome.

There was room for Roberts in Pleasant Valley; though the Graham and Tewksbury families were already established under the Tonto rim, at first they let him alone. He became friendly with the Tewksbury boys. Then some of Jim's horses began to disappear. At first he attributed the thefts to sideline activities of some of the riders out beyond.

A thousand different tales of the events leading up to and through the bloody Graham-Tewksbury feud have been told. No two stories entirely agree. I thought I saw a chance to get the real facts from Jim Roberts himself when he became a deputized watchman at Clarkdale in 1927. He was then one of the last two or three survivors of the war. I was mistaken. He could not be persuaded to talk, beyond saying that all the stories he had read of the Tonto Basin war were wrong in detail. Some day he would give the true story, he said; a motion picture company was going to pay him for it. But he wouldn't tell it now.

The most common story is that the feud started when the Grahams, cattlemen, rebelled when the Tewksburys moved a large herd of sheep into the basin. A different story was told me by my good friend the late A. B. Peach of Clarkdale.

Al Peach was a native of Pleasant Valley, having been born there under a pine tree before his rancher father had built his cabin. He became a close friend of Ed Tewksbury, who told Peach that the Tewksburys had raised sheep in the valley even before the cattlemen had settled there, and that at the time the shooting started they were preparing to increase their cattle herd and dispose of the sheep. The Grahams, Peach declared, were testy and troublesome and started the feud over a comparatively minor incident. That's a Tewksbury version.

As to Roberts' closeness of mouth, Peach told me that he knew Jim well; that he had associated with him and had taken prospecting trips with him; but that he had not learned until I told him that Roberts had been an active participant in the Pleasant Valley war.

In any case, Jim got into it, though not with any desire to fight for fighting's sake. The climax came when he found that his fine stallion and two mares had been stolen. Roberts trailed them to the rim and found them in possession of three men he had seen with the Grahams. He killed all three. There was no turning back then, and he took the Tewksbury side.

The war lasted through 1885 and 1886. It was bloody; the casualties were very high for such a thinly populated area. McClintock in his history of Arizona said old timers knew of twenty-nine men who had been killed, twenty-two of them being members of the Graham faction. How many casualties Jim Roberts' gun accounted for no one will ever know. He was as silent to the members of his own family as to others.

Roberts was really a mild mannered man, and had no earmarks of the gunman. His own skimpy records which his son William H. Roberts allowed me to inspect, show that in 1889 he was appointed a deputy by Yavapai County's new sheriff, William O. (Buckey) O'Neill, and assigned to the gold mining camp of Congress. In 1891 he was reappointed by Sheriff J. R. Lowery, and transferred to Jerome. That year he married Permelia Kirkland, whom he had met and wooed in Congress. The couple had three sons and two daughters.

In 1904 Roberts accepted a position as deputy sheriff of Cochise County, and in subsequent years ranched and mined and kept the peace.

The Verde became well acquainted with him again in the late years of his life. In 1927 he returned as a deputized watchman for the United Verde, stationed at Clarkdale. Tom Rynning, famed captain of the "twenty-six men", the Arizona rangers, had held the same job before him. It was at the age of seventy that Jim Roberts' last gun battle was fought.

The late David O. Saunders, at the time of his death in 1960 Arizona's state bank examiner, was manager of the Clarkdale bank when on the morning of June 21, 1928, he returned to the bank from a trip to the post office to find two gunmen standing guard over Bob Southard, Marion Marston and Margaret Connor, teller and clerks, and several early customers. Saunders was ordered to join them while the bank's cash was stuffed into a gunny sack. After $40,000 had been taken all present were ordered into the vault. As the heavy door was being closed Saunders told the robbers that to lock them in would mean death to all of them in thirty minutes, and a mass murder would be added to their crime. Finally the robbers were argued into closing and latching the outside grating door only.

The two robbers then left the bank, entering an open car at the curb,

As they went through the outer door Saunders began working on the lock of the grating door, and succeeded in opening it. He rushed out of the vault, seized a gun from under the desk by the teller's window, and ran outside. The robbers were then in their car a hundred feet away, and making a turn at the cross street. Saunders ran down the walk, firing rapidly.

At the time of the robbery Jim Roberts was on one of his rounds, but for some reason that he could not definitely explain he had reversed his routine course and was at the corner of the block when Saunders began shooting. As the car turned the corner the man beside the driver began firing at Jim. He missed, and the car began to gather speed.

Deliberately Jim raised his gun and took aim at the driver of the retreating car, firing twice. The man's hands fell away from the wheel, and the car swerved, turned into a school yard, and brought up against a power line pole guy wire. The man who had done the shooting leaped from the car and began to run, but a workman near by sped after him and brought him down with a flying tackle.

The driver of the car was dead, shot through the neck.

The captured man was Earl Nelson, the dead man Willard Forrester. Both men had been involved in bank robberies in Oklahoma.

Before the coroner's jury, of which I was a member, Saunders testified that Jim Roberts had fired the fatal bullet. Jim Roberts testified that he did not know which of them had killed Forrester.

The papers had a field day after this affair, and many stories, real and colored, were revived of the fabled Jim Roberts, gunfighter and lawman. Jim took it calmly, told the many reporters who came to see him nothing at all, and continued to walk his beat.

James F. Roberts, one of the "last men" of the Pleasant Valley war — a man ready to uphold the law by quiet means if possible but by violence when necessary — died with his boots on one January morning in 1934 while on his morning beat in Clarkdale. He had lived seventy-six years. His wife survived him by twenty years, but now she lies beside him in Clarkdale's Valley View cemetery.

Other lawmen in a later period in Jerome's existence gained more than local fame, but Jim Roberts will be best remembered.

Lawman Jim Roberts, far right, talks to businessmen on Main Street. (Jerome Historical Society)

Lawman from Cochise

FRED HAWKINS

Tombstone's roaring days were over when Fred Hawkins came to Jerome from down Cochise way. He was deputy to Frank Ferguson, Jerome's first marshal after the town's incorporation in 1899.

Fred Hawkins was a slender and wiry man on the tallish side. His hair was reddish in color, and he had a well weathered complexion to match. A sandy moustache drooped a bit on either side of his mouth.

He had the coldest eyes I have ever seen in any man. He didn't look at you exactly — he looked right through you. I had the feeling that whatever was behind me, Fred could see it.

Yet when off duty and among acquaintances he showed another side. He could be friendly and considerate. Toward his family he showed affection.

Eventually Fred became town marshal, and was a peace officer in Jerome as marshal, deputy sheriff or policeman for twenty years.

Fred Hawkins didn't kill unless he had to. He would disarm a man if he could, wound him if that would subdue him, or kill him if he must.

On one occasion he trailed a man into the hills horseback, and there followed a battle among the rocks. Fred walked back to town leading his horse, the dead man slung across his saddle.

Once there was a shooting affair down on the Hogback, in which a man was severely wounded. Hawkins went after the gunman, and when he refused to surrender shot him in the shoulder. After serving a year in Yuma the man came back to Jerome, and boasted that he was going to kill Fred Hawkins. He shouldn't ought to have done that, an old timer said. Hawkins trailed him down to the Wigwam saloon, where he was told he was holed up in a back room. Hawkins ordered him to throw out his gun, but instead he started shooting wildly. Hawkins shot twice; one bullet entered the ex-convict's head, the other his heart.

On another occasion a young Mexican who had been sent to the penitentiary for a shooting affair returned to Jerome to find the woman with whom he had been living prior to his departure had taken another man. Number one ordered number two to depart, pronto, or he would wind up dead. Number two told Fred Hawkins of the threat, and the marshal looked up the ex-convict to give him orders to keep the peace of the town. He took a shot at Fred, and missed. Fred didn't miss.

Help a man — you'll feel kindly toward him. Help a woman — love may come. It came to Fred Hawkins that way in Jerome. In the big Masonic building there was a fine opera house, and many traveling shows came to give plays or operas or other types of performances there. One of the musical shows which had been billed was not given because the troupe had been disbanded before reaching Jerome. One member did come, though; a singer and pianist had been separated from the troupe because of illness, and was to have met the others at Jerome. She arrived to find herself alone and in rather a desperate situation, for her funds were so low she did not have enough money to buy a ticket back to her home town in the East.

She found Fred Hawkins' ear a sympathetic one. He found her a room in a respectable boarding house. He offered to raise the money to buy her a ticket; she said please, find me work so I can earn the money myself. Fred Hawkins told her that the only place to find work in her line, singing or piano playing, would be in a saloon. Neither of them liked the idea, but the girl agreed to give it a try. The best of the saloons was the Fashion; Fred approached Hoover, of the Hoover and Cordiner partnership, and when the saloon keeper hedged the officer bent upon him a look that brought a quick response.

"Bring her in," Hoover said. "Let's see what she can do."

The girl was pretty and had a good voice; she sang the old songs with melody and feeling. She fingered the ivories expertly, too. Hoover said he'd put her on for a couple of weeks.

She was evidently of good breeding. A saloon engagement was unpleasant for her, but with Fred's help it was endurable. The officer escorted her to and from the saloon each evening, and during her performances hovered near by; no man dared to attempt familiarity. When she had earned enough money to take her home Fred told her he would not let her go, and by that time she was content to stay with him. They were married. They adopted a daughter. The wife taught music and became a respected member of the Jerome community.

The affair which brought Fred Hawkins the greatest publicity occurred in July, 1918. There had been violence in Jerome. The Wobblies were back in greater force than prior to the deportation, and were trying to promote a strike. There was unrest in other quarters. The mine was heavily guarded, and the United States government sent in an undercover man and a deputy marshal, for it was war time and there must be no interference with the production of copper.

We go back a year or two. The Second Reich was preparing for unrestricted submarine warfare; Arthur Zimmerman, German minister of foreign affairs, had sent a coded telegram to the German minister in Mexico notifying him of this intent. He instructed the minister to inform the president that in case the United States entered the war on the side of the Reich's enemies the Republic of Mexico should join Germany in a declaration of war against the United States, Mexico's reward to be recovery of their lost territory in New Mexico, Arizona and Texas.

The British intercepted the message; they had broken the German code, and delivered the contents of the telegram to the United States. The knowledge of Germany's intentions had a vital part in bringing the United States into the first world war.

Though the Mexican government did not take the bait the knowledge of the German offer inflamed the minds of a certain element among the Mexican nationals. In Jerome was a man named Hernandez, who it was later claimed had been a lieutenant in the army of Francisco Villa. He became the leader of a dissident group which had alliance with other revolutionaries in Mexico and the United States.

In July of 1918 Fred Hawkins was a special deputy working with Joe Crowley, Jerome chief of police. He knew something was in the wind. Various rumors had been floating about. Mexicans had been buying pistols and ammunition in the valley hardware stores. The reason for this was reported to Hawkins in a strange way.

Hernandez and two companions had called upon a countryman at his house in the gulch to discuss details of an uprising. An eleven year old daughter overheard the plot. Worried, and feeling the need of letting someone else know about the scheme, she visited a woman who had taught her class in school and told her this story:

On some night soon — the girl did not know when — the plotters planned to kill the town officers and mine guards, rob the banks at Jerome, Clarkdale and Clemenceau, seize the powder magazines at the mines at Jerome and the two valley smelters, then sabotage the mine shafts and the smelter power houses. They had a hundred men, fifty at Jerome and others in the valley, and they could count on the Wobblies to supply some men.

The teacher hurried up town and repeated this weird story to Fred Hawkins. Unlikely as it would seem that such a plot could exist, Hawkins took the story seriously, for it could explain mysterious activities of which he had been aware. He reported the plot to Robert E. Tally. Company officials were alerted at Clarkdale and the UVX mine and smelter at Jerome and Clemenceau. Guards were increased at all properties. Four machine guns and a quantity of Winchester rifles and Colt automatic pistols, with cases of ammunition, were obtained with government cooperation and shipped in by special service.

From a confidential source Tally received a tip on the date the revolutionists planned to strike. Everything was made as ready as could be. A warning whisper went out to the American citizens; scarcely a house in the three towns was not guarded at night by the tenants with loaded rifles, shotguns or pistols at their sides.

Fred Hawkins received a tip that on the night of the strike bombs would be set off in various places to add to the confusion. He alerted all officers. One man was caught planting a bomb; locations of other bombs were sweated out of him. They were found and removed.

There was rather a formidable list of officers of the law in the Verde Valley at that time. Frank Bartlett, an experienced officer who had been special agent for the Santa Fe, was chief of the deputized watchmen at the United Verde. Jim Lowery and John Munds, former sheriffs, occupied similar posts at the UVX mine and smelter. Bob Robbins, deputy and later to become sheriff of the county, was at Clarkdale with a corps of deputized watchmen. In Jerome, where the rumored uprising was expected to be centered, were Fred Hawkins, John Hudgens his first assistant, chief of police Jack Crowley and a city policeman named Kirby. Joe Young, county sheriff, came over from Prescott to lend aid and advice. Harry Carlson, deputy United States marshal and Crowe, under cover man for the government, were on hand.

Armed men occupied every roof in the business section, and others were within the buildings.

Hernandez knew that his plot had become known, but he had gone too far to withdraw. Most of his confederates felt differently, but he ordered them out on pain of death. But only a few of them actually took part. On the night of the uprising five of his faithful men were sent up to the mine, where they managed to set the depot on fire as a diversion in order that they might reach the powder magazine. Watchman Horace Harrison spotted the five men and accosted them. Shooting began; watchmen were believed to have shot at each other. In the melee Harrison was killed. John Hudgens was on the scene by then, and he was a man to be afraid of. The men escaped on foot to the lower valley.

Meanwhile Hernandez, his courage fortified by a marijuana cigaret, was trying to assemble his men down town. He came up from the gulch near the UVX mine, several men with him. They encountered a deputy and killed him. They then sneaked up past the cribs to Hull Avenue and on to Main Street. Fred Hawkins called to them from a doorway. Bullets flew.

Down from the roof tops the guns began to blaze. Chief Crowley and Harry Carlson joined the fight. That was too much for the remnants of the Hernandez army; they broke and fled.

"General" Hernandez was left to conduct the revolution alone. A bullet from his pistol creased Crowley's scalp, temporarily removing him from the battle. Harry Carlson was shot in the thigh, and put out of commission. Hawkins advanced upon Hernandez, who broke and ran down Main Street, headed for the river.

With Hawkins hot on his trail, Hernandez fled to the rear of a school building which stood at the top of the steep road leading from the Hogback. He concealed himself in a drainage ditch. It was dark down there. Hawkins knew from the silence that Hernandez must have come to rest. He inched forward on his belly. He dared make no sound which would betray his actual position, but he could make sound in another way. He tossed a rock down the hillside, and Hernandez blazed away in the direction of the noise made when the rock struck the ground.

Hernandez fired two shots, but that was all. Guided by the gun flashes, Hawkins shot the revolutionist through the head.

Thus the great uprising ended, completely crushed. The final word was Fred's.

The five men who had started the violence at the mine were trailed down the valley. Three of them were caught near Camp Verde, and brought back to Clarkdale and jailed. One of them was tracked by a Coconino County officer into the red rock country and killed. The fifth man was not apprehended. The Yavapai County attorney considered there was not sufficient evidence to bring the three captured men to trial for murder or arson, and they were released.

It was not long afterward that Hawkins was involved in the arrest of an employee of the United Verde who was accused of molesting a woman. This met with such strong disapproval from Robert E. Tally that they brought about Fred's discharge. That ended his career as an officer of the law. Jim Douglas gave him a job at the UVX; then he was employed to surpervise an oil drilling venture at Holbrook, Arizona, for a company composed mainly of Jerome men. While on a motor trip to California on company business he was subjected to exposure which brought on an attack of pneumonia, from which he died.

Jim Douglas bought the widow a house in Jerome, but ordered that she was to know the gift was from him. It was given her, she was told, by friends in tribute to a fine officer, a man who had done his best to keep the peace of Jerome.

A funeral in Jerome's early days (c. 1903).

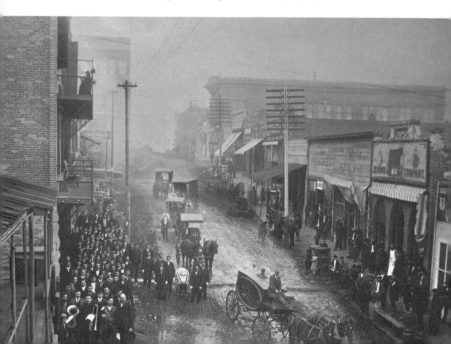

John L. Munds, Yavapai County Sheriff, 1898.
(Jerome Historical Society, McMillan Col.)

JOHNNY HUDGENS

Lawman from New Mexico

JOHN HUDGENS

They called Roberts "Jim", Hawkins "Fred", and John Hudgens "Johnny". One simply could not imagine a Jimmy Roberts or a Freddy Hawkins, but there was something of a boyish look about Hudgens that made the name Johnny seem appropriate. The was nothing of the boy about him when he was on the trail of a killer, though. Then his blood was ice water and his eyes frosty cold.

He was born in New Mexico and got his training as a peace officer in Nevada. After serving as chief of police at Ely he developed a health condition which sent him down to Arizona. He served as deputy sheriff under George Ruffner, during which time he gained some distinction by taking single handed a holed-up desperado. When Fred Hawkins' deputy Charlie King was murdered he was called to Jerome to take King's place.

I have the story of an old timer, a foreman at the mine shops who lived in Jerome during Jerome's most turbulent days, about the coming of Johnny Hudgens to Jerome and the reception he got. There had been bad blood between Charlie King and some of the Mexicans in the gulch below the town. One night — this was about 1912, the old timer said — a fight was started in what was known as Mexican Town down toward the UVX mine. Someone sent a boy up town to find Charlie King and tell him to come down and stop the ruckus. Charlie went, and recklessly opened the door of the house where it was said the fighting was going on. He was met by a blast of gunfire and instantly killed.

When Hudgens arrived Fred Hawkins did not minimize the danger he would be entering, and Johnny realized this fully when he received a note that if he didn't get off the police force within ten days he would get just what Charlie King got. Johnny stayed on, and it wasn't long before an attempt was made on his life. The enemy didn't even change the pattern. One night a boy came to Hudgens with the story of a fight in the gulch, and the good men down there wanted him to stop it.

Hudgens sensed a trap. He told the messenger to go on home, that he would be down presently. He set out, armed with a double barrel shotgun as well as the two pistols he always carried — an automatic Colt with a cartridge in the breech and eight in a clip, and a revolver. He took an indirect route, coming down back of the house and along the side to a front corner. He threw a handful of gravel at the steps of the door, and no sooner had the rattle of the gravel come than a gun blasted through a crack in the door, which then opened to show the figure of a man. Johnny let go with both barrels.

He received another note the next day telling that now he was sure to die unless he got out of town pronto.

About a week later the foreman stopped at a hardware store on Main Street to make a purchase, and found four men there buying forty-five caliber pistols and ammunition. As he left there he met Johnny Hudgens and told him about the men.

"All right, Tom," Johnny said. "You just clear out, fast."

The deputy went out to the middle of the street and waited. Soon the men came out, and seeing Johnny they started shooting. Johnny, a gun in each hand, dropped three of them. The fourth man turned and ran, Johnny in hot pursuit. The fugitive ran through a saloon and started down the hill. He attempted another shot at Johnny as he started down after him, to be met with a bullet in the head. It had taken Hudgens less than five minutes to kill all four of his attackers.

Another incident, talked of for many a day, occurred when Dave Schreiber, a tough miner with a record for misdeeds who had sought refuge in the isolation of this mining camp, tangled with a young bar keeper named Vogel who worked for an uncle, Hank Vogel, owner of a saloon between the Fashion and the Bartlett Hotel. He had come off shift one afternoon in a foul mood after a fight with his shift boss. He had come off second best and had been fired. He had warned the boss that he would kill him, and he meant to keep his promise.

He stopped in his room at the Montana Hotel, washed the blood from his face, then took a pistol from his valise and concealed it under his coat. Down town he entered the Fashion and had a drink, and waited for the shift boss who usually stopped there for a beer on his way home. The boss didn't show, and Schreiber went looking for him at Vogel's. Young Vogel was behind the bar. As well as being a bully Schreiber was a cadger, and found no welcome when he demanded whiskey. But a drink was poured.

DICK LAWRENCE PHOTO

Crumbling ruins of Jerome's famous "traveling jail." Its movement down the slope was caused by shifting and settling of surface over underground workings.

"Leave the bottle on the bar," Schreiber ordered.

"No more till you've paid your bill."

Schreiber reached across the bar, gathered in a handful of Vogel's shirt, and struck him in the face. The bartender reached for a gun he kept under the bar; as he came up with it Schreiber shot him through the heart.

The miner glared around at the few other men in the saloon. All were frozen to their stools or chairs. He hurried up to the hotel and stuffed his few belongings in the valise.

In the meantime Johnny Hudgens, who had been down the hill disarming a couple of ladies at the Cuban Queen's house who were trying to carve each other up with butcher knives, received word of the killing and followed Schreiber up to the hotel. Ed Kurmeier, the hotel manager, was tending desk.

"You know where Schreiber is?" Johnny asked.

"Right behind you," Schreiber's voice called from the stairway. As Johnny pivoted, a gun in each hand, Schreiber started shooting. A bullet struck the deputy high on the shoulder.

That made Johnny mad. He didn't like anyone to shoot at him, as he had so thoroughly demonstrated during his stay in Jerome, and he liked it less that he should be hit. He emptied both guns at Schreiber, whose gun went off twice more, harmlessly, before he crumpled and rolled down the stairs. He was D.O.A. at the bottom.

"Johnny fired nine shots from the automatic and six from his revolver," said the old timer. "One shot must have missed, for they found only fourteen holes in his body."

After the troubled war time days Johnny Hudgens went to Los Angeles, where he served as chief of patrol of Westwood for a period, then returned to Arizona to take up mining. During the second world war he worked in a ship yard at Portland, Oregon.

Johnny Hudgens was sixty-six years old when he died in Prescott in 1946 of a heart attack, leaving a widow who still survives. Members of the older generation in Jerome and the Verde Valley still like to talk of him and his exploits while helping to subdue the bad men of the billion dollar copper camp, and to compare his battles with those of Jim Roberts, Fred Hawkins, and other pioneer officers of Arizona's territorial days.

Empty buildings, lonely street, during the 1960s.

Ramshackle home (now demolished).

The general executives, with the operating officials and department heads of the United Verde's smelter, railroad and utilities divisions, at the end of the "roaring twenties" and prior to the long shutdown and the regime of Phelps Dodge Corporation.

FRONT ROW, Left to Right– A. I. Greenwood, Chief Electrician; J. E. McLean, Railroad Superintendent; C. R. Kuzell, Smelter Superintendent; W. V. DeCamp, General Manager; Robert E. Tally, President; Thomas Taylor, General Smelter Superintendent; Dave Hopkins, Purchasing Agent; F. O. Tivitty, Trainmaster of Railroad; F. H. Jones, Chief Bonus Engineer. CENTER ROW– F. X. Mooney, General Foreman Reverberatory Department; George Mieyr, Master Mechanic; Frank Avis, Chief Power Engineer; J. J. Williams, General Smelter Foreman; A. L. Reese, Chief Chemist; H. P. Hughes, Auditor of Railroad; J. R. Marston, Metallurgist; P. C. Keefe, Crushing Plant Superintendent; R. K. Daffey, Chief Clerk; P. C. Steinel, Traffic Manager. BACK ROW– L. M. Barker, Concentrator Superintendent; **H. V. Young, Secretary to the President***; F. H. Parsons, Assistant Smelter Superintendent; J. E. Lanning, Chief Mechanical Engineer; D. L. Bouse, General Storekeeper; J. C. Harding, Safety and Employment Engineer; D. L. Bouse, General Storekeeper; A. N. Jones, Superintendent, Upper Verde Public Utilities Company; Dr. I. F. Walsh, Physician and Surgeon; O. C. Ralston, Director of Research.

Addenda

OTHER MEN OF THE MINES REMEMBERED

By the time this writer began gathering material for the first editions of GHOSTS OF CLEOPATRA HILL, the names and activities of some of the men who had been prominent in Jerome's early days had become legend. Through the distribution of the book many contacts were made which became the source of additional information of value; in 1967 the Arizona State Department of Library and Archives gathered together and placed on microfilm all known issues of Jerome newspapers and news bulletins from 1895 to 1942, which were scanned; and through personal acquaintances and correspondence we have been able to collect other information. From the results of these efforts we are presenting here some information not heretofore generally known of men who helped guide the destinies of Jerome's two great mines—men not previously introduced in the pages either of GHOSTS OF CLEOPATRA HILL or THEY CAME TO JEROME.

Many rumors have been passed down from early residents and through published stories regarding the activities of the men who brought the United Verde into being, such as the perennially repeated story that Eugene Jerome would not buy shares or assist in the organization of the company unless the camp were named for him. There were other tales of like incredibility. About twenty-five years after the United Verde had produced its first copper, James A. Macdonald, the company's first president, gave Charles W. Clark some history written by the man who consolidated the various mining claims and organized the company. Clark gave the story to the Jerome Mining News, which printed it on February 8, 1908. Because of its historical value this is considered to be an appropriate spot to record the fabled Frederick F. Thomas's story of the United Verde's beginnings. It is briefed from a longer version, but nothing of historical relevance has been omitted.

The executives, operating officials and department heads of the United Verde Copper Company's mines division in 1930.

FRONT ROW, Left to Right:—O. A. Glaeser, Safety and Ventilation Engineer; J. C. Perkins, Shovel Superintendent; J. F. Couley, Planning Engineer; J. R. Allen, Shovel Foreman; W. J. Flood, Underground Construction Foreman; C. E. Mills, Assistant Mine Superintendent and Chief Engineer; W. V. DeCamp, General Manager; T. W. Quayle, Mine Superintendent.

CENTER ROW:—Denny O'Neill, Division Foreman; Frost L. Benham, Superintendent, Utilities Company; Walter Matz, Division Foreman; Paul Alloman, Chief Chemist; C. S. P. Gardner, Chief Timekeeper; H. V. Kruse, Chief Mechanical Engineer; Thomas Dennison, Fire Chief.

BACK ROW:—Dr. A. C. Carlton, Chief Surgeon; M. J. O'Boyle, Division Foreman; M. A. Heckey, Division Foreman; E. M. J. Alenius, Chief Engineer, Shovel Department; M. G. Hanson, Chief Geologist; C. I. Thomas, Mine Foreman; W. H. Riddle, Master Mechanic; F. W. Fredell, Chief Electrician.

THE REAL DISCOVERERS OF THE UNITED VERDE MINE

By

FREDERICK F. THOMAS

When F. A. Tritle was appointed governor of Arizona in 1882, he appointed me as mining expert to go to Arizona to look up paying or payable mining properties. Either late in the winter or early in the spring of 1882 I went to Prescott and became acquainted with nearly everyone in that town.

I examined everything presented or heard of within a hundred miles or more of Prescott. I was looking particularly for copper ores. One day a man by the name of Angus McKinnon told me he and his brother had a fine copper mine out in the Black Hills, about twenty-five miles from Prescott which he would be willing to bond. The next day we rode horseback over trails across the Black Hills to Angus and John McKinnon's Wade Hampton claim. There was only a log cabin there, and in it I enjoyed the McKinnon boys' hospitality.

I liked the Wade Hampton property and surroundings. The McKinnons agreed to give a six months' bond on the property if they were paid $500 cash and $15,000 on the expiration of the bond. We were also to employ them at $4.00 per day each while the bond ran. On my return to Prescott the $500 was paid and a bond given in my name for $15,000 running six months to December 1, 1882.

I went back to the Wade Hampton and put a small force to work in the mine and directed the work underground, which was not much on account of foul air, but more particularly because the owners were afraid of knocking the bottom out of the 45-foot shaft and spoiling a really good prospect. This fear I did not share.

While at the Wade Hampton I examined and sampled the Eureka. All of the samples carried more or less silver and high grade copper, and with a furnace for the Wade Hampton there was enough ore in sight at the Eureka to afford paying a high price for the mine. It was then I made up my mind that all the mines in the immediate neighborhood ought to be consolidated and handled by our company. I was taken to see the Hermit claim owned by M. A. Ruffner and one or both of the McKinnons. As there was very rich ore at that prospect and the mass was of good width, I thought it ought to be tied up and so bonded this property at what I thought was a big price at the time. I have forgotten the amount. I also bonded a claim which took in the Hermit spring and an old cabin, the property of Ruffner. Also while in the district I found out the owners of the different claims in the vicinity. Judge Riley of Nevada, an old friend of mine, owned the two Chromes, the two Azures and the Venture, I think, in connection with two nephews by the name of Dougherty and a Mr. Barry. There may have been other owners but all of the claims were bonded. We also acquired title to the spring in Walnut Gulch that supplied the water for the smelter and an engine, through a pipe subsequently laid to the works when erected. There were eleven claims in all, I believe—the Wade Hampton, the Eureka, North and South Chrome, North and South Azure, the Hermit, the Venture, the Hermit Spring claim, and two others north and east of the Wade Hampton and the North Chrome. All of these claims were finally included in one general incorporation.

I made two trips to Philadelphia to see Mr. Chas. Lennig, owner of the Eureka mine. He told me the claim had cost him $105,000–$93,000 purchase price and the balance for work on the claim and getting patent, etc.

I proposed, when we had gathered all the mines in one group and incorporated, to call the company the United Verde Copper Company as the mines were situated in the Verde District.

As the bond on the Wade Hampton was to expire on December 1, 1882, the McKinnon brothers agreed to extend the time upon my promise of payment of $7,500 by January 1, 1883, the balance to be paid three months thereafter.

I arrived at the Gilsey House in New York on December 23rd. My trip soon began to look like a wild goose chase. Moneyed men were all out of town on account of the approaching holidays. Mr. W. B. Murray, an associate of Governor Tritle in mining ventures, was waiting at the hotel. He had been trying to place the property, but as he had not seen it he had uphill work. He had only the promise of a friend in Tombstone, a Mr. Clapp, to put $1,000 in the venture. Mr. Eugene Jerome had also promised to invest $1,000, and as he told me on being introduced that the investment would not matter, as it was not his little all.

I found out from Mr. Jerome, who was a lawyer, that we could not incorporate on bonds under the laws of New York State as we must have some property to incorporate on; but he said if we paid $7,500 for half of the Wade Hampton we would have a basis for incorporation and could then go ahead.

The next proposition was to raise the $7,500 by January 1st. Mr. Murray and I then planned to give a joint note for that amount, for 60 days, and to make it attractive for acceptors we agreed to pay a high rate of interest or furnish 7,500 shares at $1.00 in a general incorporation of 300,000 shares, which should include the Eureka mine and all the other bonded claims. We succeeded in raising the money at the first application, telegraphed it to Prescott on time, and astonished the McKinnon brothers with our promptness.

At the Gilsey House I met an old college friend, Mr. Bushnell, and told him why I was in New York. He said off-hand he would take ten thousand, "just the same as if I were betting on a horse race, and I'll never squeal if I lose." I also met Mr. Edward K. Searles, who was living in the hotel. The scheme seemed very attractive to him after I had shown him the ores, and he asked me how much he ought to take—5, 10, 15, 20 or 25 thousand shares. I said, "Oh, perhaps 5,000 shares, just as if you were betting on a horse race," using Mr. Bushnell's expression. When I found out afterward how slow was the work of raising money, I regretted not insisting on his taking 25,000 shares. Mr. Macdonald told me he would take stock, and Mr. Jerome and his family considered taking a large amount.

I proposed that we call the townsite I had surveyed after Eugene Jerome, and Mr. Murray, who was his cousin, cordially acquiesced.

At this point we seemed to stick in our efforts to raise money; but with the aid of Mr. Macdonald, Mr. Henry Butler, and Mr. Jerome, we succeeded in placing the stock. Mr. Lennig bonded the Eureka mine to us for 20,000 shares of stock and $75,000 at six percent payable in six months; also he agreed that when we raised $50,000 for working capital he would add $10,000 more. That was the working capital.

The Corporation was launched with James A. Macdonald, President, and Eugene Jerome, Secretary and Treasurer. F. F. Thomas was appointed by the board of directors Superintendent and General Manager, and was authorized to purchase furnaces, water pipe, coke and supplies, build a wagon road to the property and operate it as accredited agent.

I left New York on the 23rd of March, 1883, having been engaged three months in placing the properties. Usually I do not hear my name mentioned in connection with the property, but had it proved a failure I would have been notorious.

I purchased the first pipe of Crane Brothers in Chicago, and Fraser and Chalmers, under my direction, made the first two water jackets. I built the wagon road from Sanders to the mine and opened up the mine and built a second wagon road over the mountains during my administration. The first 50-ton furnace made phenomenal runs on oxidized ores, unusually good in silver. The last work was to erect a second 50-ton smelter. We closed down temporarily, waiting for a rise in copper, but the price kept falling.

Through my old friend and schoolmate R. A. Elmer, second assistant postmaster general, I had the first post office established at Jerome and the first mail route established into the camp.

(Signed) F. F. Thomas

FREDERICK F. THOMAS

When gathering historical material for GHOSTS OF CLEOPATRA HILL I was puzzled and disappointed at my inability to find anything but scraps here and there relative to the career of Frederick F. Thomas. Yet the paucity of news about him really is not so strange when one considers that he was in Arizona only a short time. He examined the United Verde claims in 1882; in but little over a year he had consolidated the properties, raised capital, constructed a smelter, and was producing copper, gold and silver—an amazing feat considering the mines were in rugged mountains sixty miles from a railroad. Within another year the smelter and mines were closed, the United Verde was in financial difficulties, and Frederick Thomas was gone from Arizona, where no one seemed to know. His acquaintances in Arizona almost altogether were those with whom he had done business.

I knew only one person who had ever known Thomas. That was Charles D. Willard of Cottonwood, who had sold farm and dairy products in the United Verde camp while Thomas was there. He said Fred Thomas was "a very fine gentleman."

One afternoon while sitting at my desk in the Clarkdale town hall I heard someone enter, and looked up to see a tall, gray haired gentleman, distinguished in appearance.

"I am Frederick F. Thomas," he said. My astonishment must have been quite obvious. He laughed, and added, "Junior."

He was visiting Jerome to see the place which his father had named and had such an important part in putting on the map, and hearing that I was collecting historical material on early Jerome gave me the courtesy of a call.

He told me about his father. Frederick F. Thomas had graduated from Yale and the Sheffield Scientific School with degrees which qualified him to enter the mining field as an expert. He gained experience in mining first in California, then in Nevada where he met Frederick A. Tritle and William B. Murray. Tritle, after being appointed territorial governor, brought Thomas to Arizona to search for mining properties in which he might invest.

After his separation from the United Verde Thomas resumed his profession as a consulting mining and metallurgical engineer. In that capacity he was engaged in 1892 by the Central Mines in the famous Broken Hills district in New South Wales. There he developed metallurgical processes for reduction of the ores.

After returning to the United States he took charge of the Gwin mine in California's Calaveras County. Later he became manager of the Kennedy gold mine at Jackson, California, which was the last position he held in the mining field before his death in 1916.

Prior to coming to Arizona from Nevada Thomas managed the Ward mine near Ely, from which he rode horseback each week end to be with his wife and four children. Frederick Junior was born after his father left Arizona. At the time of his visit with me he was associated with a firm of prominent attorneys with offices in San Francisco and Los Angeles.

JOSEPH L. GIROUX

Every resident of Jerome is familiar with the name Giroux, because it is the name of one of the city's best known streets. But few who live in this historical area know anything about the man for whom the street was named.

Joseph L. Giroux was William A. Clark's superintendent for the Jerome mine and smelter from 1888 to 1904. During those sixteen years a "fine new smelter" had replaced the little two-furnace operation which Clark found on the property when he became owner, and the mine had been developed to the point that the United Verde had a capacity of fifty million pounds of copper a year.

Giroux was a tall, well built man, reserved of manner, heavily moustached. He was of French Canadian extraction, born in Montreal in 1854. His family moved to Illinois when he was ten years of age. When he was old enough to take a job he worked on a railroad for a time, then decided he would like mining better and obtained work in a Michigan mine. As did so many young men of the time, he got western fever and traveled to Utah, where he worked at other mines for a time then went prospecting on his own. Not finding the bonanza he sought he moved on to Montana, and at twenty-four years of age he went to work for William A. Clark.

Though without formal education in mining and metallurgy, Giroux proved to have a natural ability in solving the everyday problems of underground mining, while absorbing a store of practical knowledge relating to orebodies and mining methods. He caught Clark's eye, and in the ten years he worked in Clark's Butte mines he was advanced from miner to superintendent.

After taking an option on a majority of United Verde shares in early 1888, Clark took Giroux with him to Jerome to inspect the property. Giroux advised him to exercise his option. According to one account Clark said he would if Giroux would take over the management of the mine and smelter. Giroux agreed.

"No wonder the former operators ran out of good ore," he reported to Clark after giving the mine a careful examination. "They were working in the wrong direction."

He refurbished and started up the little smelter, developed more ores, made a profit from the operation, vastly increased when the railroad came and the new smelter fired up its furnaces.

Giroux resigned in 1904 after H. J. Allen's death and Will L. Clark replaced him. He felt that if he were to attain his ambition of operating a mine of his own he had better get at it. He acquired mining properties in Nevada and organized the Giroux Consolidated Mines Company with headquarters at Kimberly. Its properties eventually became a part of the Kennecott Mining Company's operations.

In his later years Joseph L. Giroux resided in Hollywood and Burbank, California. He died in 1933.

I am indebted to Mr. Ronald J. Giroux of Reno, Nevada, son of Joseph L. Giroux, for most of the information given in the foregoing sketch.

THE MITCHELL BROTHERS

Very little can be learned about these three men from the copper smelters of Wales. When Clark's new Jerome smelter swung into operation and Clark sent out a call for experienced smelter men, the Mitchells came.

GEORGE appears to have been the dominant one of the three. At the turn of the century he was smelter superintendent for a time, then resigned to take charge of smelting operations for the Green-Cananea Copper Company in Mexico.

ROBERT took his place at the Jerome smelter, but it was not long before George sent for him and he too went to Mexico.

HARRY then was given a whack at the management, and was around until Tom Taylor took over. Maybe he went to Mexico too.

This information is from the memories of old timers, reported during years past.

WILLIAM McDERMOTT

"I have never had a failure. I have been successful in all my undertakings." So claimed William McDermott, "Captain Billy," after engaging for more than thirty years in mining, milling, construction and railroad building at numerous properties, some his own and some owned by others. He claimed to have built the first mill in Butte, Montana, and that through his various activities he had placed that town on the map. In a promotion pamphlet for Hull Copper Company, for which he had been appointed consulting engineer, it was stated that "McDermott is the greatest superintendent of mines America has produced," and that "he is best known as the man who made the United Verde." Also that "this shy, calm man most truthfully could exclaim 'Jerome–I am Jerome!'"

William McDermott was born in 1850 in Milwaukee of Irish immigrant parents. At age twenty-two he started his career on a railroad construction crew in Dakota. From there he went to Montana. His education in mining began when he was called upon, as an expert timber framer, to do a job of underground timbering.

He was called "Captain" Billy because Cornish miners called their supervisor "Captain." McDermott kept the title, carrying it with him to Arizona.

After experience in mining he was employed by William A. Clark to search for promising coal and mineral properties in Utah and Nevada; then when Clark started his Salt Lake, Los Angeles and San Pedro railroad he put McDermott in charge of construction. When Joseph Giroux resigned as mine superintendent at Jerome Clark brought in McDermott to take his place.

McDermott has been quoted as saying development in search of ores at the United Verde mine had been pursued in the wrong direction, and that by exploring in the right direction he found more ore.

Mrs. McDermott didn't like Jerome. When McDermott was offered the superintendency at a better salary of the Twin Butte mine near Tucson he accepted. It was, he said, a more favorable location in which to raise and educate their children.

Quoting from McDermott's biography in McClintock's history:

After nearly three years with the Twin Buttes Company, where he made a success, as he has always done in other places, he became interested in real estate in Tucson and mining properties of his own, and having some spare time and of active mind, began to look around to see what could be done to improve Tucson. He was president of the Chamber of Commerce, and through his influence and work more than any other one man Tucson today is a city of the first class and he is still doing things too numerous to mention, and as he says "you can't keep a good man down."

"Captain Billy" McDermott died in 1937 in Los Angeles, where he had moved. A son, Morgan McDermott, had served in the first World War, and was killed the day before the war ended. Tucson's first American Legion post was named for him.

THOMAS W. THOMAS

Not very much is known about William A. Clark's third mine superintendent at Jerome. A hard-working practical miner, he was handed the mantle of the top hand on the operating force when William McDermott resigned in 1907.

His reign was brief. A year later he was dead.

Tommy Thomas, as he was known, was born in Cornwall, England, in 1868. As a lad he gained experience in the mines there. In 1889 he came to America, and as a miner in Butte, Montana, he continued his chosen occupation.

He was working underground in one of William A. Clark's mines when an offer was made to underground miners to travel down to the United Verde in Arizona and take jobs there. At that time the Jerome mine was just swinging into production. Giroux picked Thomas as a good man to watch, and under his aegis the Cornishman advanced from miner to shift boss, and from shift boss to mine foreman. When Giroux left Thomas was considered capable of stepping into his mentor's shoes.

When he died in 1908 twenty-nine year old Robert E. Tally was given a chance to prove whether a young college man could operate a mine, which some of the old time hard rock miners doubted. He was given the title of assistant mine superintendent under Will L. Clark.

Instead of laying him to rest in Cemetery Hill, Tommy Thomas's Masonic brothers buried him in Cottonwood's graveyard.

Clarence V. Hopkins, United Verde Copper Company Chief Engineer.

CLARENCE V. HOPKINS

He was born in Butte, Montana, in 1880. After attending grade and high school in Butte he studied mining engineering at the Michigan School of Mines, from which he graduated in 1901 with degrees of Engineer of Mines and Bachelor of Science.

During a period of service with the United States Geological Survey, where he developed skills as a surveyor, he attracted the attention of Senator Clark's keen eye. The Senator employed him and sent him down to Jerome, specifically for the purpose of surveying mining properties, underground as well as on the surface.

He established a reputation for accuracy. The greatest test of his skill came in 1906 when the United Verde executives decided on the construction of a waste haulage and drainage tunnel from the 1,000 foot level of the mine to an exit on the mountainside a mile and a quarter eastward from the new shaft which was also involved in the project. Hopkins, who had been promoted to chief mining engineer was in charge of this work. After the completion of the shaft he started the excavation of the tunnel from both ends, from the shaft and down on the side of the mountain, the aim being to meet in the middle. There was considerable speculation as to whether or not it would be possible to engineer the project accurately enough to join the two halves of the tunnel evenly. It took twenty-one months to complete the work—and then, according to the Jerome Mining News, the engineering had been so accurate that "levels at the juncture of the two sections did not vary three-eighths of an inch."

Hopkins also did studies on Verde Valley water, and was an authority on the flow of the Verde River and adjacent springs:

He directed the surveying for the new Clarkdale smelter and town sites in 1912.

On account of illness Clarence Hopkins resigned from United Verde service following the post-war shutdown in 1920 and 1921. He moved with his family to California. There he became a licensed surveyor for the State of California, and at the time of his death in 1945 he was a safety engineer for that state.

He was survived by three children, Robert, Clarence Junior, and Dorothy.

Exit of Hopewell tunnel, which Clarence Hopkins built from "both ends to the middle." Above, mule power used in building. Below, the ore trains used to transport ores to the Clarkdale smelter, 1915 and after.

CHARLES R. KUZELL

One of the main characteristics of Charles R. Kuzell was his constant search for knowledge—for an understanding not only of the forces and products of Nature, but of man-made products and processes as well; what they were, why they were, and how they could be made better. This applied particularly to the sciences with which he chose to associate himself.

Charles Kuzell was born in Cleveland, Ohio, in 1889. His father was an immigrant from Bohemia who, with the drive that later characterized his son, overcame all obstacles to become a successful lawyer.

The son chose as his life work the fields of mining and metallurgy. After graduation from a Cleveland high school he enrolled with the Case School of Applied Science. In 1910 he received the Degree of Bachelor of Science in Mining Engineering, and in 1914 he was awarded the advanced degree of Metallurgical Engineer.

He began his career in mining and metallurgy as assistant metallurgist for the Anaconda Mining Company in Great Falls, Montana. In 1918 the United Verde Copper Company borrowed him from Anaconda to assist in the testing and installation of equipment for making powdered coal and using it in the ore smelting process. Ever on the alert for promising young ralent, Robert E. Tally obtained his release from Anaconda.

From metallurgist Kuzell was advanced successively to assistant smelter superintendent, smelter superintendent, and in 1934 general superintendent of mining and smelting operations at Jerome and Clarkdale. When Phelps Dodge Corporation took possession of United Verde in 1935 he was retained as general superintendent of the smelter and concentrating division of the United Verde branch. In 1940 he was transferred to Ajo as manager of the New Cornelia branch, but in a few months he was returned to Clarkdale to become manager of the United Verde branch, his predecessor W. M. Saben having taken early retirement.

In 1944 he was appointed director of labor relations and consulting metallurgist at Douglas. In 1946 he became assistant general manager, and from 1952 to his retirement in 1958 he served as vice president and general manager of Phelps Dodge Corporation's western operations. He retained the post of president of the Apache Powder Company, a joint operation of a group of mining companies, until 1971. In 1956 he became a member of the board of directors of Phelps Dodge Corporation. In 1968 he resigned as an active member, and became an honorary member of the board until his death in 1971.

Charles Kuzell was a member of all important technical organizations in his field of interest and took part in their activities. He never relaxed his search for new methods, and his research resulted in several patents of value to the industry.

In recognition of his contributions to the non-ferrous metallurgical industry in 1956 he was the recipient of the James Douglas Gold Medal, awarded by the American Institute of Mining, Metallurgical and Petroleum Engineers. In 1955 he received from the University of Arizona the honorary degree of Doctor of Science.

Charles R. Kuzell and Miss Theresa O'Leary were married in Great Falls in 1915. She preceded him in death. Surviving are three sons and one daughter: Dr. William Kuzell of San Francisco: Colonel Ralph Kuzell, USA Ret. of Flagstaff, Arizona: Commander Charles E. Kuzell, USN Ret. of Huntsville, Alabama; and Mrs. George J. (Mary) Niznik, of Phoenix, Arizona.

H. DEWITT SMITH

During the expansion period of the United Verde Copper Company which followed the discovery of large new ore bodies in the mine and the construction of the new Clarkdale smelter, the management extended its search for outstanding young talent in both the mining and smelting fields. One product of this search was Henry DeWitt Smith.

DeWitt, as he preferred to be called, was born in Connecticut in 1888. He studied the mining sciences at Yale University, graduating with an E. M. degree. After working as a mining engineer in Nevada and Mexico, in 1914 he entered the employ of the Kennecott Copper Corporation, and he had been advanced from foreman to assistant manager of Kennecott's Alaska mine when in 1917 he was offered and accepted the position of mine superintendent for the United Verde Copper Company, from which position he was advanced to assistant general superintendent and then, in 1924, to general superintendent of the mines division.

DeWitt Smith was interested in industrial engineering, and in 1924 he joined the staff of the New York Trust Company as an engineer in its industrial department. In 1927 United Verde set up its own sales department in New York, and Smith returned to that company as manager of sales.

The depression beginning in 1929 just about stopped copper production and sales, and in 1930 Smith became an engineer for and a director of Newmont Mining Corporation. He was its vice president until his retirement in 1953, and continued as a director during his lifetime.

He had a hand in the operation of several of Newmont's mining properties. He engineered the purchase and return to production of two inoperative South African mines which returned two hundred million dollars in dividends.

During the second world war he served the United States as director of the Metals Reserve Company.

In 1935 he served as president of the American Institute of Mining, Metallurgical and Petroleum Engineers, and the following year was awarded the Institute's Charles F. Rand gold medal. He was president of the Mining and Metallurgical Society of America in 1953.

DeWitt Smith was married in 1916 to Ellen Dawson of New York City, and had three children, Charles DeWitt, Elizabeth Cass, and Jeanette. He died in 1962. In his death the engineering sciences lost a brilliant member, one who had served well not only his profession but his country.

W. VAL DeCAMP

A native of Iowa, Val DeCamp arrived in Denver, Colorado, with his parents at an early age. He attended grade and high schools in Denver, then enrolled at the Colorado School of Mines, from which he graduated with the degree of mining engineer.

In 1913 he took a position with the United Verde Copper Company at its Jerome mines, then left their employ to accept the position of mine superintendent at the Blue Bell mine of the Central Arizona Smelting Company at Mayer, Arizona. He left this post to enlist in the United States Army Engineers, in which he was commissioned first lieutenant. His duties during the first world war were confined to the United States.

Following the war DeCamp studied at Columbia University in New York, earning the degree of Master of Science. In 1920 he returned to the United Verde as general mine foreman. In 1923 he was made mine superintendent, and in 1924 upon the departure of H. DeWitt Smith he was appointed general superintendent of the mines department. When in 1928 Robert E. Tally went to New York as president of the United Verde Copper Company DeCamp was appointed assistant general manager, and in 1929 he was advanced to general manager. He was released from United Verde employment in 1932.

Subsequently he went to South America as a manager of mines for American interests. He had returned to the United States when he died at Monrovia, California, in 1944.

W. Val DeCamp and his wife, nee Margaret Hinman of Denver, had two children, born in Arizona, Rosemary and Jerry Val. Rosemary, famed actress of radio, screen and relevision, has made the name DeCamp familiar to millions in this country and far beyond.

CARL E. MILLS

Like many other young men of talent, Carl E. Mills heeded the call of the West. There he found both success and romance.

He was born in Houghton, Michigan, in 1893, and after high school he enrolled with the University of Michigan's College of Mines. He graduated from that institution in 1915 with a master's degree in engineering. That same year, after a few months experience as an underground miner in Michigan's Isle Royal mine, he accepted a position in Jerome as assistant engineer in the Mines division of the United Verde Copper Company.

He served in the United States army during World War I. In 1918 he married Miss Ynez Reynolds, a Californian who was teaching in the Jerome public schools.

After the war he returned to his work at the United Verde. There he was advanced by 1935 to mine superintendent. When Phelps Dodge Corporation took control of the United Verde properties in 1935, Carl

Mills was retained as chief engineer of the mines division; later he was advanced to mine superintendent and then to general superintendent of the United Verde branch. In 1950 he was transferred to Bisbee as assistant manager of the Copper Queen branch, and the following year he was made manager of the branch, which included supervision of all mining and smelting operations at Bisbee and Douglas. From this post he retired in 1956, to move to Carmel, California.

Carl Mills died in Carmel in 1972. Surviving were his wife and a son and daughter, Mark and Marcia, Mark, a resident of Carmel, is a talented architect, trained at Frank Lloyd Wright's famed Taliesen West near Phoenix.

THEODORE W. QUAYLE

Born in Denver, Theodore W. Quayle—"Ted" to all his acquaintances—attended grade school and high school in his native city, then enrolled with the Colorado School of Mines at Golden from which he graduated in 1907 with scholastic honors. He then embarked on a series of positions from which he gained wide experience in the field of mining.

He received his first experience in a mine in Tuzatlan, Mexico. Next he worked with the Chisos Mining Company at Terlingua, Texas, until 1915, when he took a position with Phelps Dodge Corporation at that company's Tyrone, New Mexico, branch. In 1920 he joined the staff of the New Mexico School of Mines, at Socorro as an instructor.

In 1922 he returned to Mexico with the Moctezuma Copper Company at Nacozari, Sonora. In 1924 he came to the United Verde at Jerome, advancing to mine superintendent, the position he held when he left that company's employ in 1932.

At the time of his death in 1936 Ted Quayle was engaged in placer mining in California.

His widow, Helen Geary Quayle, whom he met and married in Jerome, resides at Clarkdale, Arizona.

Down and down, level by level.

When 1,000,000 tons of rock broke away from the pit wall, burying and damaging equipment, some of the fragments were as big as a house.

WILLIAM W. LYNCH

Born in Darien, Connecticut in 1894, William ("Bill") Lynch received his early education in local schools. He then entered Phillips Academy at Andover, Massachusetts, followed by studies at Sheffield Scientific School at Yale University, from which in 1917 he received the post graduate degree of Engineer of Mines.

He learned something of what mining was all about as an underground laborer in mines of Ontario and South Dakota in the summers of 1915 and 1916, and following graduation, in 1917 and 1918 he served Kennecott Copper Corporation at an Alaskan mine as jigger boss. Then to the Army; in 1918 and 1919 he was a sergeant with the Twenty-seventh Army Engineers. After his discharge he was for six months an underground surveyor for the Whitmarsh Mining Company in Minnesota. Late in 1919 he was in Jerome as an employee of the United Verde Copper Company.

Starting as an underground surveyor, during the shutdown of 1920–1921 he was given work as an underground laborer. After surviving that test, from then to 1929 his progress was steadily upward: Planning engineer for development and stoping; assistant mine superintendent; mine superintendent; then general superintendent of the company's mines division.

In 1929 he was transferred to the New York office, where he became the manager of the company's sales department. After that office was discontinued in 1931, Lynch went to Washington to work on copper tariff matters; then down to Bolivia in 1935 to become assistant general manager, then general manager of a mine for Compania Unificada de Cerro de Potosi.

Back in the United States, from 1941 to 1944 he was assistant manager for the American Potash and Chemical Company at Trona, California. Then again with the United States government in war work with Metals Reserve and the Reconstruction Finance Corporation. Following that, until his retirement in 1959, he was with the Calumet and Hecla, Inc. in their New York offices as vice president for metal sales and procurement.

As a consulting engineer, William W. Lynch did work in 1929 and 1930 in Canada at the Frood Mine of International Nickel Company and the Lake Shore gold mine. In 1939 he engaged in general examination of several gold mines in the Philippines for a London bank.

In the writing field, in 1939 he worked on the revision of the "Mining Methods" section of Peele's handbook, and in 1960 on writing the mining section of the book "Winning of Nickel."

William W. Lynch and Miriam Baynes Hatch were married in 1918. Three children were born to them: William W., Jr., Miriam Baynes, and Ynez Whiting Lynch.

Bucketful by bucketful they tore down half a mountain.

LOUIS EHRHART REBER Jr.

The accomplishments of Louis E. Reber—"Doctor" to some, just plain "Louie" to many more—were far better known in the outside mining world than they were to the citizens of Jerome, his home for many years.

Louis Reber was born in 1889 in State College, Pennsylvania, where his father was a teacher of engineering and dean at Penn State College. After moving to Wisconsin Louis received his M.A. degree in Geology from the University of Wisconsin in 1913. A study and report on the geology of copper deposits at Morenci, Arizona, contributed to his receiving the Ph.D. degree from Yale University in 1916.

He had an inquiring and analytical mind, with powers of concentration given to but few. He worked on projects with Dr. A. N. Winchell, one of America's most prominent geologists, including a study at the Copper Chief mine at Jerome in 1916. He was employed by the United Verde Copper Company that same year, and subsequently was appointed chief geologist. He made intricate studies of the United Verde ore bodies, and made reports commended for their clarity and evidence of deep study. This culminated in the publication of one of the best known of several published studies, "Geology and Ore Bodies of the Jerome District." He was hailed by one noted geologist as the world's greatest authority on Pre-Cambrian formations.

He took a leave of absence in 1925 to conduct exploration in Africa for Newmont Mining Company and others. He was there through 1928, then returned to Jerome. After Phelps Dodge took over the United Verde in 1935, Louis worked at other branches of that company, including Copper Basin, Ajo, and Morenci. In 1954 he was returned to Jerome as general agent for the United Verde Branch, a position he held until his death in 1966.

His ability to concentrate to the exclusion of all else resulted in an absent-mindedness that was the basis for many stories still recounted in friendly spirit by a host of friends and acquaintances. A brief example: He rode horseback to inspect some claims a mile away, tied the horse to a tree, forgot it, walked back to Jerome and didn't remember it until next day.

Louis married Rachel Wieman in Jerome in 1919. She died in 1953. He is survived by a daughter, Mrs. Rachel Miller of Laguna Beach, California, five grandchildren and six great-grandchildren. He died in 1966.

Following his death the Geological Society of America published a moving memorial to Louis Ehrhart Reber, Jr. It was written by Charles A. Anderson of the United States Geological Survey. In it Mr. Anderson pays this tribute:

"Fond memories of Louie Reber, the man, will long be cherished by his many friends." He could not have spoken truer words.

A cave-in at the U. V. mine in 1898 destroyed buildings, displaced railroad track and ruined roadways. Another similar cave-in destroyed the assay office and caused casualties.

MAYER G. HANSEN

He was born in Minneapolis, Minnesota, in 1898, and graduated from the University of Minnesota's College of Mines in 1922, with an E.M. (Geology) degree. He chose the mines of Arizona in which to pursue his calling, and after brief employment with the Ray mines he came to Jerome that same year as a geologist for the United Verde Copper Company. He remained with this company for eleven years, during which time he planned the systematic mapping of the mine; he provided data for the planning of development work; he directed the diamond drilling program and drilling research. In the area of tax litigation in which the company was involved, Hansen did research on mine depletion and valuation. In addition to that, he was involved in the United Verde's search for other mines, examining various mineral properties and conducting geophysical prospecting.

He was chief geologist when he left the company's employ in 1933, in the midst of the depression and the four-year shutdown. There followed association with a number of companies in the United States and the Philippine Islands, where he served in consulting and managerial capacities. He was in Manila when Japan entered World War II, and he had a break from mining activities while being confined in the Santo Tomas internment camp in Manila from 1942 to 1945.

After the war he returned to the United States. He worked as field geologist and negotiator for Newmont Mining Corporation, then from 1947 to his retirement in 1963 he was with E. J. Longyear Company of Minneapolis in their mining division in managerial and consulting capacities. Since his retirement he has done consulting work on a private basis.

Mayer G. Hansen is the author of a number of technical pamphlets and papers.

He was married in Jerome in 1922 to Agnes M. McDonnell of Minneapolis. She died in 1972.

JOHN F. COWLEY

He lived the life of the average mining engineer, moving from mine to mine as the demands of his work dictated, each change being of advantage not only to himself but to the organization to whom he gave his services.

John Cowley—known to everyone as Jack—was born in New Hampshire in 1888. In 1900 he moved with his family to Oregon. After graduating from high school in Central Point, he enrolled with Oregon State University at Corvallis. A two year hitch in the army interrupted his studies, but he returned to graduate in 1921 as a Bachelor of Science in Mining Engineering.

Employed by the United Verde Copper Company in 1923, as an underground miner he had the chance to find out if his college training was of real value. The proof lay in the fact that he made jigger boss, then shift boss, then foreman. Finally he was promoted to the important position of planning engineer for both the underground mine and the open pit, which then was in development.

Jack left the United Verde in 1935, to take the superintendency of five mine developments in Grass Valley, California. Then he was president of the West Coast Mines in Winnemucca, Nevada, until the second world war, when he was called to Washington to work on the discovery and acquisition of strategic minerals for the government.

Next he served four years as consultant to the government of Turkey on mining problems. Then he was president of the Vermont Copper Company for seven years, and following that he became associated with the J. G. White Engineering as mines consultant, stationed in Taiwan for seven years. He then retired, in 1962 establishing a home in Jerome's neighboring town of Clarkdale. He died in 1973.

John F. Cowley was married in 1927 to Miss Joan Shea of Jerome, who survives him. Also surviving is a son, Lt. Col. John F. Cowley, Jr., U.S. Army.

Men of The UVX

GEORGE KINGDON

Uncle George"—as he was known around the mine—was another one of that dwindling breed of men who, without what is known as a formal education, made good even in a fast increasing technical age, their training obtained in the school of hard knocks.

He was a native of England, son of a farmer who had eleven other children to support. George felt his opportunities lay elsewhere, and at the age of fifteen severed family ties and headed west. He worked his way to America on a freighter. He had had enough of farming, and he liked the idea of becoming a miner. He knew of the Michigan mines; he found his way there. He got a job in a copper mine and at once set out to learn all he could about the mining business. He worked and studied hard, and was rewarded by being advanced from miner to shift boss, then to foreman, while still but shortly out of his teens.

The West continued to beckon him. He left Michigan and traveled to Arizona. There was ever the hope of fulfilling a dream—owning a mine of his own. He heard of a place where there was placer mining, in the Globe area. He acquired a prospecting outfit, complete with burro, and set out to find the gold which in his mind's eye he saw glittering out there. He found an abandoned placer claim, an old stone cabin on it.

He gave it a good try, working harder than he had ever worked before. He managed to pan subsistence wages for a time, then gave it up and took a job with a copper mine at Globe. His Michigan experience served him well; by 1908 he was superintendent of the mine.

In Globe he met and married Maude Kenyon. Together they went to Mexico, he to superintend the development of a mine in the bandit-infested Pilares district. Mrs. Kingdon later wrote a book about their experiences—"From Out the Dark Shadows"; by Maude Kenyon-King, 1925. She avoided giving dates for the most part.

177

GEORGE KINGDON
UVX General Manager

WM. J. McDERMOTT
*United Verde Superintendent
and Assistant General Manager
1904-1907*

It was in Mexico that James S. Douglas met George Kingdon, and after Douglas had struck it rich at the United Verde Extension at Jerome he sent for George, and made him general manager. Kingdon stayed until UVX passed in its chips in 1938. He and his wife then retired to a home they had waiting for them in San Diego, and there they passed the remainder of their days.

The Kingdons had no children, but they raised a niece of Mrs. Kingdon's, Audrey, as their adopted daughter.

"Uncle George" liked to be known as a man with distinctive traits. He deliberately cultivated little peculiarities. As an example, he usually stood out in a crowd because of the bright red hat he always wore, together with a red tie, the more brilliant the better.

His usual response to the greeting "How are you?" or its equivalent, was to say mournfully "Muy triste"–Spanish for "Very sad."

RICHARD L. D'ARCY

Though James S. Douglas did not hesitate to employ for positions of authority capable men without college degrees, he was just as ready to engage the services of men with university training if they appeared to have promise.

Such a man was Richard L. D'Arcy. Born in Denver in 1882, he attended the Colorado School of Mines, graduating in 1905. He worked in the mines of Goldfield, Nevada, until he entered the employ of the United Verde Extension Mining Company at Jerome in 1916.

Engaged as a mining engineer, he progressed to chief engineer, then to superintendent of mines, a position he held until UVX expired as a producer in 1938.

With Alfred B. Peach he did some mining under lease at the UVX underground mine for a short time, after which he retired with his family to his home in Clarkdale.

Richard D'Arcy married Blanche Wall in 1907. Four daughters were born to the couple, Genevieve, Mary, Frances and Clara.

D'Arcy died in 1966, Mrs. D'Arcy in 1970.

CLARENCE JOSEPH BEALE

Clarence Beale came to be one of the best known men in Jerome and the Verde Valley during his residence in the mining city of more than half a century.

He was a forceful character, and no one ever had any doubt as to where he stood on any subject. He spoke his thoughts in a deep voice charged with pungent vocables that reverberated through any room or hall in which he might be. While others hesitated, he spoke. While others pondered, he declared.

Clarence Beale was born in Yonkers, New York, in 1878. He attended public school in Peeksville, New York, He then enrolled in Peeksville Academy, where his stay was temporary, then successively in several other prep schools in New York and New Jersey, from each of which he was separated by stern faced preceptors of academe without asking his advice or consent.

He took a business course in New York, then headed westward, arriving in Denver in 1900. After working at several mines in New Mexico and Arizona, in 1910 he went to Cananea, Mexico, to work for James S. Douglas, then manager of the Green-Cananea Copper Company as head of the timekeeping department. That position he held until 1920, when Douglas brought him to Jerome to serve as chief accountant and superintendent of labor relations.

After the United Verde Extension mine and smelter were closed in 1938 and UVX became Verde Exploration, Beale stayed on as agent for the owners, a position he held until he was 90 years old.

He served three terms as a member of the board of trustees of the Mingus Union high school. The athletic field of this high school at Clarkdale was named for him.

Volatile, peppery, lovable Clarence Joseph Beale died in 1972 in his ninety-fourth year.

Other UVX Officials

DAVE MORGAN

During the period of search and discovery at the United Verde Extension mine, Dave Morgan was superintendent.

GEORGE W. PRINCE

He was smelter superintendent at Clemenceau during the greater part of the smelter's operating life.

JOHN C. SALISBURY

He was supervisor of the smelting operation during the final period of the UVX operations, ending in 1938.

ROSS D. LIESK

First employed in 1919 as an engineer, Mr. Liesk served as Assistant General Manager from 1926-1936. He greatly contributed to the development of its bonanza mine.

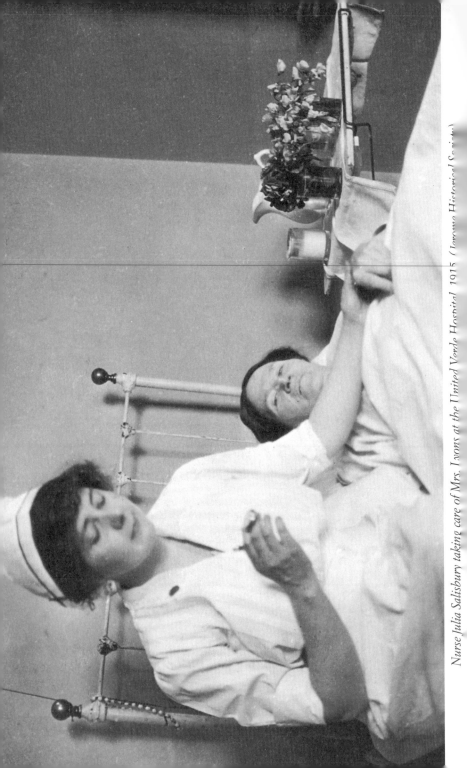

Nurse Julia Salisbury taking care of Mrs. Lyons at the United Verde Hospital, 1915 (Jerome Historical Society)

Women of Cleopatra Hill

BY ALENE ALDER

Women were the civilizers of wild western towns and Jerome was no exception. When miners first moved into the area and began staking claims, few women accompanied them. Most wives remained behind to take care of families, while their men ventured out to strike it rich. However, women soon followed men to the billion dollar copper camp. And, despite their important role in the everyday life of Jerome, women have received little recognition from historians.

Women always ranked as a minority in Jerome during the mining era. The 1900 census only records 22% of the population as female. By 1910, that statistic had risen to 28%, and in 1920, it was 36%.

The scarcity of women created a ready market for prostitutes. Many of the first women to arrive consisted of those of low moral standards that were willing to provide sexual services for the lonely miners. Madams rank among Jerome's most notorious women. However, most of the identities of the prostitutes remain completely lost. A few of their names appear in arrest records. Only two women listed their profession as "prostitute" in the 1900 census, and none did so in later censuses. The census takers did not record most of the prostitutes or listed that profession as something else.

Jennie Bauters is known as Jerome's most notorious madam. She ran a brothel on Main Street that had "cribs," behind the building. Cribs were small rooms where the low-priced ladies lived and worked. Jennie owned fine clothes, furs and jewelry. When the devastating fires of 1897, 1898 and 1899 destroyed her building, she quickly rebuilt. Her last building was of fine stone and brick, which still stands. Jennie was the first in the business district to build a sidewalk in front of her establishment. She had a reputation for being a generous soul and was always charming to her customers. Jennie left Jerome in 1902 for Gold Road, near Kingman, where she was killed by Clement C. Leigh, whom they eventually hung for her murder.

Prostitution was illegal, but generally tolerated in the mining camp. Periodically Jerome's law enforcement officers went on a crusade to clean up Jerome by forcing the prostitutes out. Often, the women were charged with vagrancy or with being an "inmate of a house of ill repute." The courts fined them ten to fifty dollars. The women usually paid and went back to work. If they were unable to pay, they could leave town. Yet, brothels remained and flourished in Jerome throughout the mining period.

As wooden and brick buildings replaced tents, wives replaced ladies-of-the-night as the majority of women in town. These women brought the standards of civilized Victorian culture to Jerome, and eventually helped to push the wilder women to the fringes of Jerome society.

The home was considered women's proper domain. The U.S. censuses between 1900 and 1920 list stay-at-home mothers as "none" under employed, which only means they did not receive salaries for their labor. They did, however, work. Maintaining a proper home and taking care of children was a full-time job. The soot from the smelters made cleaning a daily necessity. Keeping laundry clean after spending an entire day washing it was nearly impossible. In winter, the clothes froze solid on the line.

One housewife, who moved her family to Jerome in 1903, was Della Margarite Geary. Her first impression of Jerome was, "a place God forgot." Mrs. Geary was born July 4, 1863 in New York to parents of Irish descent. Before her marriage, she owned a fashion designer shop in Chicago. After marrying Patrick F. Geary, they relocated to Denver. Later he moved to Jerome and found work as a foreman in the United Verde smelter. He left his wife behind in Denver. Unsatisfied with this arrangement, Mrs. Geary packed up her four children, including a newborn baby, and set out for Jerome, without notifying her husband. After the frightening trip over the rickety narrow gauge railroad, they arrived in Jerome near the end of a shift. Her daughter, Helen Geary Quayle, recalled this experience:

> When we got into Jerome, the men were just being let off shift. And my mother sat on the company store steps across from the Fashion Saloon. All these ugly miners, all different nationalities, bearded and everything. She sat on those steps and cried bitterly. My father standing there terribly embarrassed. Pretty soon a group of saloon girls, dressed as can-can dancers with roses in their hair, with paint and powder on came out and did a dance. Oh and I was just thrilled to pieces. I thought they were so beautiful. I

clapped and jumped up and down. Every time they would sing I
would clap. I never saw anything so marvelous. My mother said
"Helen if you jump up and down and holler and yell and clap once
more I am going to smack you right here in front of everyone." So
I quieted down. I made up my mind that when I grew up I was
going to be a saloon singer. (Helen Geary Quayle, Interview 1977)

After Mrs. Geary got over the initial shock, she set about finding her
family a proper home. The only thing available to purchase, for $300,
was a one room windowless shack near the Clark Street School. Mrs.
Geary made the best of it. When she could not find a carpenter to put
in windows, she did it herself, and even added a front porch that she
screened with chicken wire to keep the baby out of trouble.

Settled into their new home, everything was going well for the family. The children were in school and Helen was taking piano lessons from
Mrs. Fred Hawkins. In 1907, however, disaster struck when the children
became ill with scarlet fever. The Geary's lost three children within a
month. "That broke my mother's heart." Helen Geary Quayle recalled:

My mother had two little caskets in her living room at the same
time. My father was up in the rectory of the Catholic Church with
the priest, prostrate with grief. He didn't know what in the world
to do. He had brought his family to such a place. (Helen Geary
Quayle, Interview 1977)

They packed up the remaining two children and fled to Denver, but
returned to Jerome about a year later. Mrs. Geary did not want to live
away from her dead children. The family later moved to Clarkdale, to
the area now called Geary Heights, where she lived until her death from
pneumonia on April 1, 1930.

Mrs. Geary's story illustrates the hardships that many women faced
in Jerome as they tried to make a proper home for their families. Jerome,
in its early days, was not a healthy place for children. Disease spread
quickly because of the cramped living quarters and poor sanitation. A
high childhood mortality rate was not unique to Jerome, but the poor air
quality, caused by the smelter, exacerbated the problem.

Mothers tried to protect their children from the harmful moral
influences of the seedier side of Jerome. Before moving to Jerome,
Mrs. Geary had never been in close contact with saloon girls, but her
daughter, Helen, ended up being influenced by contact with them. She
became a singer and dancer and played in theaters throughout the country.

Mabel K. Schrepel with daughters Ardith, Marianna and Betty Ruth.
(Jerome Historical Society, Callaway Col.)

Class was a major influence in women's lives. This was usually based on their husbands' occupations. Wives of muckers and miners had to scrape to get by, whereas wives of engineers and foremen lived lives of relative luxury.

Wealthier women that resided on Company Hill had servants to help take care of their homes. The elite entertained themselves by forming their own social groups. They sponsored dances and operas. In addition, they campaigned for funds for church and social charities.

Ann Doherty Hopkins was a woman of Jerome's high society who went astray. She lived in Jerome from 1904 until 1921. In her autobiography, she describes her three children, all born in Jerome, as the most important things in her life. Her marriage to United Verde Copper Company's Chief Engineer, Clarence V. Hopkins, was unhappy but gave her social standing. As a daughter of poor Irish immigrants, Mrs. Hopkins accomplished her social ascent through the "college of hard knocks." She felt a strong distaste for Jerome society, keeping her vow to "never become part of it." Mrs. Hopkins did not stay within her social parameters. She became involved with working class affairs such as the 1917 strike. Like others of her class, her writings' illustrate elitism. She felt that the Jerome school system contained too many foreign children that could not speak English. She sent her children to St. Joseph's Academy in Prescott, Arizona. Unlike most married women of the early twentieth century, Mrs. Hopkins controlled her own finances. She saved money and purchased real estate in Jerome and Clemenceau. This financial independence exacerbated the tensions in the marriage. Her marriage and life fell apart in 1921. Unable to tolerate the rumors of her husband's infidelity with a Jerome school teacher, Mrs. Hopkins broke down. On March 31, 1921, Mrs. Hopkins attacked Miss Lucille Gallagher, the other woman, with carbolic acid.

> Without a word of accusation or warning, Mrs. C. V. Hopkins walked up to the table in the Hotel Connor restaurant at Jerome where Miss Lucille Gallagher was eating her breakfast about 8:30 this morning, and dashed a tumbler of carbolic acid in the girl's face. (The Prescott Evening Courier, March 31, 1921.)

Society instantly turned against this upper class lady. She was sentenced to 5 to 15 years in the state penitentiary. This sentence was extremely harsh in an era when women would often receive a light sentence for murder.

Although below the elite class of Ann Hopkins, Tottie Skidmore was an example of a Jerome housewife who lived a life of relative comfort. Her husband, Frank Skidmore, worked in the warehouse of the United Verde Extension. Before moving to Jerome in 1923, Frank had worked for other mining companies throughout the Southwest and Mexico. Between 1923 and 1936, the couple lived on the Hogback in various company owned houses, which they rented for $25 a month. According to Frank's U.V.X. Employment card, he made $150 a month. Mrs. Skidmore recalled his wage as even more. The Skidmores had resided in Cananea, Mexico where they became accustomed to having servants. In

Jerome, they could not afford them so Mrs. Skidmore took complete responsibility for tending house and taking care of the children. She still found time for social activities. The ladies from the U.V.X. socialized with each other, played bridge and crocheted. Mrs. Skidmore was an active member of the Eastern Star. She also enjoyed tennis and swimming. Several housewives from Jerome formed a basketball team that practiced against the Jerome High School students. Mrs. Skidmore considered her time in Jerome very enjoyable and comfortable.

Many poorer women found life in Jerome a hardship. Much of Jerome's population consisted of immigrants from all over the world. Mexicans made up the largest group of foreign-born residents. Others came from Italy, Croatia, Serbia, Ireland, Scandinavia, Russia, Canada, Britain, Greece, Spain, Germany, and elsewhere. One did not need skills or even English to find employment in the copper mines. Men often came to America and worked for several years before bringing their wives over. Young unmarried men, after working in the mines, would return to the old country to find a bride and bring her to Jerome.

Jim Cambrusi immigrated to the United States in the early 1920s. The oldest of 13 children, he had to send money back to Italy to support his parents and younger siblings. In July 1933, he returned to Fonzason, Italy to find a bride and married Margaret Fusinato, ten years his junior. When they arrived in Jerome as newlyweds on Halloween 1933, Mr. Cambrusi's friends greeted them with a great fanfare. He rode a burro from the railroad station to Jerome, while she piled into a truck. This was quite an experience for the young bride who spoke no English.

Things were very different in Jerome than in Italy, although the large population of immigrants from all over the world helped Mrs. Cambrusi feel less out of place. She quickly picked up Spanish and some English from her neighbors. Spanish came easier due to its similarity to Italian. She did not learn to read English until her oldest daughter, Nina, began school. Nina would bring home her beginning reading books so mother and daughter could learn to read English together. This helped Mrs. Cambrusi obtain her American citizenship papers when her oldest daughter was about eight.

Most miners' wives had to struggle to make a good home for their family on their husbands' meager wages. They found themselves in shacks or apartment houses barely fit for family living. Many immigrant women could not speak English. Their children learned English at school and their husbands at work. But, in their isolated ethnic neighborhoods, women had little opportunity to pick up the language.

Many immigrant women, like Maria Svob, kept boarders to supplement family income. Maria Kauzlarich Svob was born in 1879 in Belo Selo, Croatia, Austria-Hungary, one of seven children. As a child, she was responsible for helping with household chores. Unable to attend school, Maria learned to read and write by observing her brother do his homework. After coming to America, she also learned to read and write in English. With the encouragement and financial support of her older brother, Maria's parents decided to send their daughter to American in hopes of a better life than their poverty-stricken country could provide. She boarded the ship Panonia in 1904 to sail to Ellis Island. Unable to speak the language she carried a note that explained her destination. From New York, she traveled to Ohio where her brother was supposed to meet her, however, upon arrival Maria discovered her brother had died a week before. She found employment as a housekeeper until she could join her sister in Albia, Iowa. There she met and married Ignac Svob in 1905. They moved to Missouri and then to Jerome. Her husband, also Croatian, found employment with the United Verde Copper Company as a miner. After years underground, the Company made him a watchman. He worked faithfully for the U.V.C.C. until his untimely death from silicosis in 1937. The Svobs raised nine children in Jerome on a miner's wage, and instilled in them the value of hard work.

Some women could not afford to stay at home. The majority of employed women were single, widowed, or separated. Other women found that their husbands' salaries could not support their families. Only a small minority of professional women worked outside their homes.

The 1920 United States Census for Jerome shows 11% of women as employed outside the home in forty different professions. These professions included housekeeper, laundress, clerk, boarding house keeper, waitress, teacher, and nurse. Women also found employment as stenographers, dressmakers, telephone operators, and hairdressers. Some worked as traffic managers for the mine company, others as musicians, dental assistants, jewelers and printers.

Since women were usually paid less than men for their labor, single mothers found it very difficult to make ends meet. They had to balance caring for their homes and children with outside employment. The prejudice against working women did not make life any easier. Despite these difficulties, many women lived without husbands. This was partially due to high mortality in the mines. Also, some couples separated when the women refused to move on with their husbands.

Melena Metzlers, separated from her husband, raised four children on her own. She cleaned people's houses and took in laundry, in addition to running the Mountain View Boarding House. Her children helped as much as they could. Laura Williams remembers her mother struggling and scrimping to support her family by herself.

According to the 1920 United States Census, the most common occupations for women in Jerome were housekeeper and laundress. These jobs involved tasks that women were expected to do for their families anyway. When times got tough, women used their domestic skills to earn wages.

Most women that were listed as housekeepers on the 1920 census were widows or were separated from their husbands. The majority of housekeepers did not live at their place of employment. They traveled to the homes of the wealthy for work.

The large number of single men created a high demand for laundresses. However, because doing laundry was a menial, labor-intensive job, it was reserved for Chinese men or lower class women. Most laundresses in Jerome were widowed or separated African-American or Hispanic women. Since they could usually bring laundry home to wash, it was a good job to combine with childcare obligations.

Running a boarding house was another choice available to women. The high influx of single men that needed places to live and someone to prepare their meals made this a viable option. Boarding houses ranged from just a few miners living with a family to large establishments like the Boyd Hotel. Women operated or assisted with most of these the hotels and rooming houses.

Kitty Christian Boyd Cain was one of Jerome's most successful female hotel proprietors. Born on July 16, 1862, Kitty Christian moved to Jerome in 1889 to be with her sister Mrs. John McKinnon. Here, she met and married miner John D. Boyd. He was killed while working in Mayer, Arizona soon after their marriage. She returned to Jerome with her young son, Fred, and established the St. Charles Hotel. After it burned in 1897, she built the brick Boyd Hotel that still stands on Main Street. Harry Cain, a mining engineer, whom she married in 1898, quit his job to help her run the hotel. The property, however, remained in her name. In 1899, Mrs. Cain was the fourth largest landowner in Jerome; at her death in 1930, she owned $50,000 in property.

Jerome offered more opportunities for employment to single women than to their married sisters. They were not burdened with the social prejudice against working wives or the stress of balancing childcare obligations with outside employment. Employment was considered a proper thing for a young lady until she found a husband. Because of the disproportionate amount of single men to women, Jerome was an excellent place for a young woman find a mate. Single women worked as clerks, waitresses, teachers, in the post office, and as nurses.

Women were employed in shops during the mining era. Men were usually the proprietors of businesses. Wives of small business owners worked alongside their husbands. Many paid employees in shops were single women. Men generally did not want these jobs because they could make more money working for the mine companies.

Jerome had a variety of restaurants. Women found employment at these establishments as managers, cooks, and waitresses. When Nellie Thomas moved to Jerome from Missouri to live with her married sister Cora Reimer, she found employment as a waitress at the Montana Hotel. However, she found the crude manners of many miners disconcerting and moved to Wickenburg to work at a Harvey House, until she saved enough to go to California.

For educated women, there were opportunities such as teaching and nursing. Jerome had an excellent school system. Still, the turnover in teachers was high. The high attrition was due mostly to marriage. Society viewed teaching as the perfect career for bright, educated young women prior to marriage. Teachers in Jerome socialized with the single mining engineers. Once marriage took place women usually quit teaching. However, the 1920 census lists four married female teachers.

Some teachers chose never to marry. As teachers, they had their own personal income and social standing. Alta Fogal was one such woman. She was born in Tempe, Arizona in 1898 to Frank and Alice McBrayer Fogal. She received her teaching degree from Tempe Normal School and B.A. degrees from Arizona State Teachers College and Colorado State College. She taught in Jerome for 22 years, and served as Principal for 17 of those. Miss Fogal was active in the Jerome Business and Professional Women's Club. She became its state president in 1928.

Jerome School Teachers, 1913. (Jerome Historical Society, Buckley Col.)

While the doctors get most of the attention in medical histories, the hospitals could not have operated without dedicated nurses. Jerome's most famous nurse was Martha (Mattie) Leyel. Her family settled in Clarkdale in 1912 when she was ten years old. She decided she wanted to be a nurse at age 15 during the influenza epidemic. After completing her nurses training at Los Angeles General, she began working at the Jerome Hospital. During much of her 20 years in Jerome Mrs. Leyel served as surgical nurse and head nurse. In 1945, she helped found the Lawrence Memorial Hospital in Cottonwood. Her marriage to Solven Leyel, a mine engineer, early in her career did not stop her from following her chosen career.

> In Clarkdale, I had my first nursing experience during the big influenza epidemic that swept the world in 1918 killing millions of people. I was fifteen years old. I worked all summer helping care for patients housed in the temporary infirmary, which had been set up in the ballroom of the clubhouse. The mining company built beds for the patients, and when there was no more room, they built tent houses with more beds. The food was prepared in the

clubhouse kitchen. As I recall, we made mustard plasters in the
kitchen also. (Martha Leyel, Autobiography)

Jerome had two women newspaper editors. Laura Nihell ran the
Jerome Copper Belt and Edith Whitiker was a partner in the *Jerome Sun*.
Both women supported unpopular causes, which damaged their careers.

Mrs. Nihell purchased the *Jerome Copper Belt* from Frank and Ralph
Smith in 1909. When Bill Adams, publisher of Jerome's *The Jerome
Mining News*, began to print editorials that accused the Chinese restau-
rant owners of unsanitary practices, Mrs. Nihell became their defender.
The two editors ran direct attacks against each other. Mr. Adams printed a crude cartoon that blatantly mocked Mrs. Nihell's support of the
Chinese. Mrs. Nihell's son could not tolerate this attack on his mother's
honor and retaliated by publically assaulting Mr. Adams. This ended the
dispute. Mrs. Nihell continued publishing her paper until 1912 when
the *Jerome Copper Belt* and *The Jerome Mining News* consolidated.

Edith Whitaker joined Lindley C. Branson as co-owner and editor of
the *Jerome Sun* in 1916. Her family had a homestead in Jerome's
Deception Gulch. Miss Whitaker ranks as one of Jerome's most maver-
ick women. She enjoyed working on and riding her own motorcycle.
Although she had many gentlemen callers, she found none to her liking.
Her involvement in the *Jerome Sun* fit her rebellious personality. The
editors of the *Sun* strongly condemned the practices of the United Verde
Mine Company, the primary employer and landowner in Jerome.
Whitaker and Branson accused the company of corruption and of con-
trolling Jerome's town council. Eventually these attacks become intoler-
able and the United Verde forced the *Jerome Sun* out of business.

Professional women in Jerome banded together to form the Business
and Professional Women's Club. The members included teachers, nurses, stenographers, clerks, telephone operators, and insurance agents.
Other members included married women that had formerly worked in
those professions. They met monthly for dinner and bridge. The
Business and Professional Women's Club gave a Bride's Dinner to cele-
brate marriages of those members that had found mates. They helped
other young professionals by providing scholarships and mentoring.
Two members of Jerome's Business and Professional Women's Club,
Alta Fogal and Emma Brosam went on to become presidents of the
Arizona Federation of Business and Professional Women's Club. The
City of Jerome hosted their conventions in 1927 and 1938.

Although women could not work in the underground mines, their economic and social role was significant. They took care of homes and families and worked in support industries. Women have always been central to Jerome's well-being and they should be recognized as such.

BIBLIOGRAPHY

1900 United States Census for Jerome, Arizona.

1910 United States Census for Jerome, Arizona.

1920 United States Census for Jerome, Arizona.

Antenelli, Nina Cambrusi. Interview by Alene Alder, November, 2000, Jerome Historical Society Archives.

Frederick, Mark C. "Cough, Gasp, Wheeze: The Role of Disease in Jerome's Past" *The Jerome Chronicle: Quarterly of the Jerome Historical Society* (Fall, 2000), 7.

Hopkins, Ann. *The Answer.* Unpublished manuscript, 1934. Jerome Historical Society Archives.

Justice Court Records, 1912 to 1913, Jerome Arizona, Jerome Historical Society Archives.

Kostrenich, Richard. "The Svob Family" manuscript, Jerome Historical Society Archives.

Leyel, Martha. Interview, Jerome Historical Society, D-90-144.

Leyel, Martha. "Autobiography" Jerome Historical Society, D-90-144.

Newell, Winifried. To Jerome Historical Society, letter written June 10, 1998. D-98-66.

The Prescott Evening Courier, Prescott Arizona, 1921.

Quayle, Helen Geary. Interview, Cottonwood Library, 1977, Sarah Bauquet two tapes, Jerome Historical Society D-90-470.

Reisdorfer, Kathryn. "In a Moment of Rage: The Ann Hopkins Story" *The Jerome Chronicle,* Summer 2000, Jerome Historical Society.

Skidmore, Tottie Louise. Interview by Nancy Smith, April 8, 1988 tape recording with notes. Jerome Historical Society, D-90-340.

Smith, Nancy R. "Jerome's Billion Dollar Boom, Bustle and Bust" *Experience Jerome and the Verde Valley: Legends and Legacies.* Sedona: Thorne Enterprises, 1990.

Smith, Nancy R. "Women in the Herstory of Jerome" presented at Yavapai County Community College, Clarkdale, AZ. March 18, 1997.

Vecchio, Janolyn Lo. "Alta Fogal" *Arizona Federation of Business and Professional Women's Club.*

Verde Copper News (Jerome), Jerome Historical Society Archives.

Westcott, Roberta Blazina. Interview by Alene Alder, November 29, 2000, Jerome Historical Society Archives.

Williams, Laura. Interviewed, June 13, 1978. Transcript. Jerome Historical Society, Jerome, AZ. D-90-36.

Young, Herbert V. *They Came to Jerome.* Jerome Historical Society. 1972.

Some of Jerome's permanent residents.

DICK LAWRENCE PHOTO

Post Script

In previous editions of GHOSTS OF CLEOPATRA HILL, it was stated that much of Jerome's history was yet to be written.

In my second book on the Jerome scene, THEY CAME TO JEROME, published in 1972, a part of the indicated chore was done in the writing of the story of Jerome itself and of its people.

While both books dealt with the early history of this mountain camp, its mines and its inhabitants, there remains to be told the detailed story of Jerome after the great depression of the early thirties, the long shutdown of the mines and smelters, the departure from the scene of the storied Clark and Douglas families, the hiatus caused by the final closing of the big mines, the advent and reign of Phelps Dodge Corporation, the descent of the camp to a genuine ghost city—and then the arousing of the few remaining citizens to the fever which resulted in the transformation of Jerome to one of the major tourist attractions of America.

This is a fascinating story that must be told, and if the author of this book cannot accomplish it, there are those who can, men and women who have lived in Jerome during this period and still live there. Written either by an individual or in community, the full story then will have been told of this fascinating and colorful spot on the Arizona map once described as "the most unique city in America."

ADIOS

INDEX